LEADING THROUGH
UNCERTAINTY

EMOTIONAL RESILIENCE
AND HUMAN CONNECTION
IN A PERFORMANCE-DRIVEN WORLD

JUDE JENNISON

First published in Great Britain by Practical Inspiration
Publishing, 2018

© Jude Jennison, 2018
Photos © John Cleary Photography, used by kind permission

The moral rights of the author have been asserted

ISBN 978-1-788-60019-4

Practical Inspiration
PUBLISHING

To my sister Sue

Who provides stability and wisdom in moments
of extreme uncertainty

PRAISE FOR THE BOOK

No one can deny the uncertainty we each face daily. Jude's insights, drawn from both business settings and working with horses, replace a fear of uncertainty with a sense of hope and opportunity. Her stories inspire; her insights inform; and her tips encourage change. Through her work with horses, Jude has developed an intensely human capability: to help leaders recognize their style and improve its impact on others.

Dave Ulrich
Rensis Likert Professor, Ross School of
Business, University of Michigan
Partner, the RBL Group

Jude Jennison's leadership lessons show great empathy and creativity. Her ideas are fresh – and they work.

Julia Hobsbawm, OBE
Author of Fully Connected: Social Health in an Age of Overload
and Hon. Visiting Professor in Workplace Social Health, Cass
Business School, London

A thoroughly engaging, human and insightful book and definitely one for now!

Gina Lodge
CEO, Academy of Executive Coaching

Leaders transform complexity to clarity and uncertainty to understanding. Get Jude's new book to move into deeper clarity and deeper understanding to navigate change with grace, authenticity, connection and presence.

Kevin Cashman
Global Head of CEO and Executive Development, Korn Ferry
Best-selling author of Leadership from the Inside Out and The
Pause Principle

An uncertain landscape has become the one certainty for business and good leadership has become even more important. This book is for all those who want to ensure they can lead their organisations through these challenging times. Practical insight from those who've "been there, done that" and some very different approaches to the challenges of leadership.

Ian O'Donnell, MBE
Director, FSB and Head of Policy for the West Midlands
Combined Authority

Wholehearted, engaging, and compassionate. Jude Jennison's second book delivers powerful truths and insights into successful leadership in the face of uncertainty. This book positions business struggles as human struggles, allowing leaders to embrace the unknown in an embodied and authentic way in order to move through to what's next.

Dr Veronica Lac PhD
Founder of the HERD Institute and author of the book
Equine-Facilitated Psychotherapy and Learning:
The Human-Equine Relational Development (HERD) Approach

This book is a key narrative at a time when change and the implication of change has never created more pressure on leaders and leadership.

Martin Yardley
Deputy Chief Executive (Place), Coventry City Council

Humans can think, can emotionalize, they can make good decisions, they can make bad decisions, they can be creative and innovative, they can be mean and fight each other. In short, they are what they are supposed to be and do. If they 'find' the link back to their natural roots, where they belong, they have a better chance of understanding themselves and moving forward. Jude Jennison gives us these ideas through her book. By reading it, your mind will be definitely challenged!!!

Prof. Alexandros Psychogios
Professor in International Human Resources Management,
Birmingham City Business School

Jude Jennison understands the complexity of modern day leadership and the pressure leaders of today are under to perform at their very best. Jude's approach, through working with her horses, places a spotlight on your skills and ability to adapt in unfamiliar surroundings. The results are powerful and empowering. A must for anyone who is serious about being the best leader they can be.

Sue Grindrod
Chief Executive, Gower Street Estates Limited t/a Albert Dock
Liverpool

I was struck by Jude's knowledge and insights on leading through uncertainty. Her warm and engaging style brings out the best of the CEOs she has interviewed to make this a valuable book.

Sue Noyes
Non-executive Director and Former CEO, East Midlands
Ambulance Service

If you struggle with your emotions in business, if you don't dare to express your feelings, if you are suppressed by what is around you – take your time and read this book! You will probably find yourself. Definitely you will get a new perspective on leadership.

Gerhard Krebs
Founder of HorseDream and the European Association of
Horse Assisted Education

TABLE OF CONTENTS

Foreword .... *ix*

Introduction 1

Part 1: The context of uncertainty **15**
1   My path of uncertainty 17
2   Human beings vs supercomputers 25
3   Emotional engagement 39

Part 2: You are not a machine! **55**
4   Stress and overwhelm 57
5   Fear and polarisation 73
6   Pain and trauma 89

Part 3: Human connection **105**
7   Creating the framework 107
8   Co-sensing and co-shaping the future 123
9   Listening and dialogue 139
10   Connection and support 155
11   Building trust 169
12   Staying with the discomfort of uncertainty 183
13   Being human 197
14   Leading from the heart and soul 213

Epilogue *223*
Meet the equine team *225*
Acknowledgements *233*
About the author *237*

FOREWORD

Leading Through Uncertainty, Jude Jennison's second book, provides a powerful narrative and account of the increasingly fast-paced, ever-changing environment of leadership. It guides and challenges us to adapt our behaviour as leaders and to learn new skills – essential if organisations are to thrive and have an engaged, fulfilled and productive workforce in the future.

Jude shares her wisdom, built up from having had a significant career in a major corporation, and aligns the conquering of her lifelong fear of horses with the challenge of building a successful business.

Jude draws on her up-to-date research with CEOs and her experience of working with leaders and teams in this book. Using her masterful and engaging storytelling style, she offers a practical guide and a valuable source of learning. The additional resources and papers extend this learning.

While many CEOs acknowledge they work with, are comfortable with and expect uncertainty in their roles, uncertainty does bring stress. It overwhelms, brings fear, and polarises. We are all familiar with the leadership mantra, 'It is lonely at the top.'

This book guides us in the elements we need as leaders to make our teams feel safe and able to be productive, and to create structure and certainty out of chaos and confusion.

Huge advances in technology can help us if we correctly harness the power of the ability to process vast amounts of data. However, we all hear the cries of despair from people trying to manage and respond to hundreds of emails each day, while attempting to make sense and meaning from facts and figures presented in spreadsheets, databases, reports and apps. Jude highlights that we are not robots or machines but human beings whose contribution could be greater if allowed to slow down in order to speed up, which is a step towards managing the positive advances technology brings to our businesses.

We look to past data to help us predict the future, which is not really possible. Predicting trends, yes, but predicting the future is, of course, a skill we do not possess. If we are not acknowledging the difference as leaders, the level of uncertainty felt by us and our teams will soon pervade the organisations we lead. Tests are used to determine our character types. While such data is, indeed, useful, relying on it can inhibit your team's personal development and deny the human capability to adapt and change our behaviour.

As human beings we have the capability to be innovative, to develop relationships and to collaborate, and for this we need space in which to think and reflect. The truth is that most organisations and leaders are still required to be results driven, with everyone being expected to act in direct conflict with our natural gifts and abilities; we are back to trying to be the computer rather than work with it!

Much effort and financial investment is spent on improving the performance of your team. Often, the complex emotions associated with being human are overlooked and people do not engage, leading, not surprisingly, to the investment making little or no contribution or change.

Every generation learns from the past. Already there are media- and research-driven labels given to the next generation of leaders, some less complimentary from the perspective of those on the receiving end of the naming conventions. It is my experience and hope that the next generation of leaders will simply not accept the outdated leadership styles of command and control, and of chasing results alone, and will set about building trusted relationships and managing reputation better than may be the norm at present.

In *Leading Through Uncertainty* Jude states that "it takes an exceptionally skilled leader to balance the energy of driving results with the softness of nurturing in complete harmony" and in this the gauntlet of challenge is cast. This is our call to action in all organisations.

When running highly respected horse-assisted leadership, team development programmes and coaching through her company Leaders by Nature, Jude is assisted by her team of five horses: Kalle, Opus, Tiffin, Mr Blue and Gio. I am sure you will feel connected to these wonderful animals by the end of the book and will learn how they can help develop the vital leadership skill of self-awareness.

Working with horses can indeed put many out of their comfort zone and lead us to see that as soon as we, as leaders, revert to control, we have ceased to trust ourselves and our teams. We are guided in considering how leaders can have a degree of certainty in an uncertain world and how the solid backbone of values that we fall back on in times of uncertainty is key to keeping on track. We learn how to not slip back to old, potentially destructive styles of leaderships in times of uncertainty.

My own experience with horse-facilitated leadership was profound and memorable. Whether we feel fear or vulnerability, it is essential that for the sake of our organisations, teams and personal wellbeing, we find a path towards calm and effective leadership.

As Jude Jennison says: We are human after all!

Gina Lodge, CEO, Academy of Executive Coaching (AoEC)

INTRODUCTION

"What do you say and do in those moments of uncertainty? You lead. That's all you can do."

My inspiration for this book came when I was sitting in a field with my dog for four days in July 2016. I was exhausted and in a head spin with a high volume of work and continuously operating out of my comfort zone. I was clear where I was heading but unsure how to get there. I knew that what I was experiencing was common for many of my clients as the world felt more uncertain on a global scale.

I took myself off for four days, sleeping in a safari tent on a farm with only my black labrador dog, Pepsi, for company. We had the most amazing time together, hardly seeing or speaking to anyone, and the result was the title of this book.

A title may not be much output for four days' reflection, but it created a spark, and sometimes we need space for the creativity to come. I returned to work inspired, knowing that the uncertainty experienced in the world was a replica of the uncertainty that my clients and I were also experiencing.

Everything seems uncertain. Perhaps it always has. As research for this book, I interviewed CEOs from a variety of organisations and sectors.

> *Many of the CEOs I interviewed thought that uncertainty was not a new phenomenon but had become more obvious as the pace of change accelerated. They had learned to seek and create certainty amongst chaos, identify risks, prepare for them and accept the things they could not control.*

But that's easier said than done.

There are huge challenges facing leaders today. We live and work in uncertain times in an era of rapid change, driven by technology and the global economy. As people live longer and work longer, your career may span 50–60 years where previously it was about 30. In the last 50 years, we've experienced substantial change in the way we work. The next 10 years are likely to transform beyond recognition as new technology influences further the way we live and work.

Traditional forms of leadership are unsuited to addressing the current global problems of fear, polarisation and disconnection that exist in the workplace as well as the wider society. New and effective ways of leading need to evolve quickly and replace command and control, competition and hierarchy with collaboration and shared leadership. Yet few people have been trained to behave in this way. While everyone likes to think they are collaborative, few truly know how to embody it. The time for dialogue and exploring how we move forward together, embracing our differences, has never been greater. In parallel, the pressure people are under has never been more intense.

How we lead in business and the decisions we take fundamentally shape the world and society. The responsibility of leadership lies with each and every one of us.

The challenge of uncertainty

Uncertainty is uncomfortable. It is something to be embraced rather than feared, but it requires a shift in our thinking and behaviour. Uncertainty creates unforeseen opportunities if we are willing to step over the edge and out of our comfort zone. It also creates stress and overwhelm, fear and polarisation, and in those moments, you wonder whether you can continue like this. The volume of workload is overwhelming, and the fundamental desire to get everything right and be in control is not possible or sustainable.

A different approach is required in leadership. Somewhere, somehow, something has to change. You cannot meet aggressive targets in an environment of uncertainty unless something shifts.

Employees are experiencing the discomfort of leading through uncertainty. They know they need new skills, yet they don't always get the relevant development. They want to evolve, yet often they lack the appropriate support to do so. The spotlight is on them, and there seems to be little room for failing and recalibrating. It's uncomfortable and creates stress as people put inordinate pressure on themselves to "get it right". Leaders need to find a way to ease the mental and emotional load, for themselves as well as for their team. Uncertainty generates a wealth of emotions that we must face head on and accept as being part of the process. We can minimise those emotions by adapting our behaviour and developing new skills.

In addition to the pressures of work, we are human beings experiencing the challenges of life. As work and life are more integrated than ever before, the challenges we face become more difficult to balance. Life is not certain for any of us. We can plan for things as much as possible, but events will always happen outside of our control. We can choose how we respond, and our choices have consequences.

Uncertainty has a cycle. It requires a letting go of one thing so that something new can emerge. Beginnings are often uncertain because the outcome is unclear, and beginnings arise from the ending of something else. People often feel as though their back is against the wall in uncertainty, and they make decisions from that state. We are all somewhat unskilled in uncertainty, and we are all also skilled in it. We have moments when we have no idea what to do and moments when we are willing to risk everything and take a stand for what we believe in.

We spend huge amounts of time imparting knowledge, believing we need to have the answers.

Uncertainty provides an opportunity to step into "How can we…?" This is a paradigm shift from knowing to not knowing, from individual knowledge and power to collective wisdom and collaboration.

Throughout this book, I explore how leaders in organisations must recognise the human challenges that we face – in ourselves and each other – and embrace them in leadership. Challenges are here to stay. Our role as leaders is to meet those challenges with curiosity, compassion, gentleness and courage.

Horses and uncertainty

In the course of my work as an executive coach and strategic leadership partner, I bring clients to work with my herd of five horses. It may sound strange but the horses invite clients to return to their true nature while working in an environment of uncertainty and unpredictability. It provides an opportunity for people to explore how they lead out of their comfort zone. Working with horses creates an embodied experience of leadership where people flex their leadership style, find new ways of leading and increase self-awareness through feedback.

My clients work with me and the horses on the ground. No riding is involved. Once you put a rider on a horse's back, the relationship changes. When you work with a horse on the ground, it is based on pure partnership where neither party has ultimate control over what happens. It provides an environment for people to explore a different way of leading that is more relational, more collaborative, and based on engaging and inspiring others to work with you.

Horses are masters of sensing beyond the words, and they provide non-judgemental feedback on your non-verbal communication. They don't care who you are or what job you do. They want to know whether you can lead them to safety, be clear about where you are going and include them in the decision-making through a solid relationship based on trust, mutual respect, confidence and compassion. The hierarchy is definitely flat when you enter the paddock. Your negotiation skills are about to be put to their greatest test. By including horses in the exploration, people show up more fully and gain greater insights into where their leadership is in flow and where it is not, thus allowing an opportunity for recalibration throughout the day.

Research shows that in the presence of horses, you align the head, heart and gut, combining the wisdom of your intellect with your emotions and gut instinct. The human race has been trained to rely on the information in our brains, yet we have so much more wisdom in our reach. When we align the intellect with our emotions and gut instincts, we are more authentic, have more clarity and behave in a more congruent manner.

A client leading Kalle

By their very nature, horses appear to be unpredictable to most people. That's largely because we don't always understand their behaviour. As a prey animal, their primary goal is the safety of the herd. They work as a cohesive unit and share responsibility for their collective safety. They therefore provide an ideal learning environment for leading through uncertainty.

Working with horses provides an environment of uncertainty where your leadership is in the spotlight. The horses require the same qualities of a leader that a human team requires – clarity, direction and purpose, balanced with relationships based on trust and mutual respect. They need all of this to feel safe, as people do, too. Ultimately, the horses want to know that you are authentic and acting with integrity. If you create an environment that makes them feel safe, they come with you; if you don't, they plant their feet and refuse to move. Either way is feedback and a chance to recalibrate and expand your leadership capabilities by trying new approaches.

When people first meet the horses, they are often scared because they don't know whether the horses will cooperate. The sheer size and presence of horses can be intimidating and invoke anxiety. Some people say they've never met anyone bigger and stronger than them, and it immediately poses a threat. This is especially true for men, many of whom often unconsciously use their physicality to exert power, whereas women are used to not being physically the strongest in the room.

Overpowering a horse physically is not going to be the answer. Telling them what to do because you are the boss doesn't work here. Being a people pleaser won't get you a result either. The horses want to know that you can lead them through uncertainty, balancing clarity and focused action with strong relationship skills.

I often start the day by explaining that I don't know what is going to happen. The day is full of uncertainty and the unknown, and not just for the clients. I watch people shrink back at that moment. There is an expectation that as the leader of the day, at my venue with my horses, I should be "in charge" and "in control". That's a myth. I lead through uncertainty with every client. I never know how people will show up and how the horses will respond. I'm constantly flexing my approach.

The best we can hope for in any given moment is to lead and to make decisions based on the information we have available – not just intellectual information, facts and logic but also the information that we gain from our emotions and our gut instinct. Both of these provide us with great insights into what action we might want to take as a leadership choice in any given moment. Emotions and gut instinct have largely been dismissed in favour of logic and reasoning, but they are increasingly critical to the success of business.

Where are you striving to be "in control"?

What happens when you loosen your grip?

Your emotions offer an important source of information. If you are terrified when you first come face to face with a horse, it is feedback that you can use as a guide to how you might approach them and the first leading exercise. It would be foolish to put yourself into a situation that causes you to instantly reach a place of overwhelm, yet many find themselves in overwhelm in the workplace. In a moment of sheer terror, the wise option might be to ask for help, to reflect and observe or to seek more information to help guide your decision. Alternatively, if you feel relaxed when you first come face to face with a horse, then the next step of leading one is not as big a step and might take you only slightly out of your comfort zone. Part of what people learn is how to challenge themselves out of the comfort zone and how to create safety and support in doing so.

Everyone's comfort zone is different based on values, beliefs, experience, self-awareness and self-esteem, and much more. There is no right or wrong baseline, but it is interesting to know where your benchmark is.

How comfortable are you leading through uncertainty?

How much do you seek control?

People's default patterns of behaviour show up around the horses. Some clients I work with are confident with the unknown and are able to lead effectively, even if they feel anxious. Others are terrified to the point of overwhelm and need more support to achieve the same task.

> *Horses respond based on non-verbal feedback and provide a great opportunity to experience where you get out of your comfort zone and how you recover to a place of powerful leadership.*

Background to this book

My leadership career began at IBM where I worked for 16 years. I held a variety of roles in the outsourcing business, and in the latter years of my career I was regularly asked to sort something out that was unclear but needed attention, often at a European or global level. I learned how to provide clarity of direction and engage a team to work with me in some challenging senior leadership roles. Always leading through uncertainty. I did the jobs nobody wanted, creating structure and certainty out of chaos and confusion. However, it was only in 2011, when I overcame my fear of horses and started working with them, that I really understood what it took to be an effective leader in uncertainty.

This book is born out of my combined leadership experience of working in the corporate world, running a small business and especially working with horses. I draw on both my experience and my clients' experiences of working with horses to highlight the key concepts of leading through uncertainty.

Every day I lead through uncertainty.

Each time I lead a horse, I don't know whether my leadership is enough.

Will the horse come with me? Will I be safe? Am I clear enough? Is the relationship strong enough? Can I achieve what I want to achieve?

Although I don't dwell on these questions, they are always there in uncertainty. With little horse experience, I have only my leadership to fall back on. The horses will not go along with anyone or anything they don't want to. Neither will people. They may come grudgingly or unwillingly for a time, but the low levels of employee engagement in business require a step change in leadership to energise people and organisations better.

In October 2016, I brought together a group of thought leaders to explore the topic of uncertainty. I was unfazed leading through uncertainty as a result of working with horses. I noticed that many of my clients were uncomfortable with the concept of uncertainty and not knowing, yet they were experiencing it and struggling with it on a daily basis. I ran a round table and included horses in the discussion. Yes, that's right: I included horses. I stepped into uncertainty and trialled a new way of running a round-table discussion. I didn't want the discussion to be purely cognitive and intellectual. I wanted the delegates to embody the concepts we discussed and gain feedback on how we lead from a different species. Horses provide a powerful way of enabling that to happen. My intention was to challenge our thinking on leadership and learning, to expand our awareness of the leadership skills needed for the future of business and to fully embody the concepts we discussed. I wanted us to shift our thinking and create ideas through dialogue and exploration.

The output of that day was a white paper on leading through uncertainty. As I wrote the white paper, I kept true to the discussion that the group had. I wrote up each topic based on the group's collective discussion and notes, but I realised I had more to say, and it was a struggle not to include my own thoughts in the report. The report was published in November 2016, and the seed of the idea for this book was sown.

 The *Leading Through Uncertainty* white paper can be downloaded at www.judejennison.com/uncertainty

When I took ownership of my first horse in December 2011 and started delivering Equine Guided Leadership, I recognised that leaders were operating against a backdrop of uncertainty in their work. I was living and breathing it daily every time I led a horse, as leaders were in their everyday work, sometimes realising it, sometimes not. When I talked about uncertainty with clients, I observed the discomfort they had with that word. Their desire to achieve results meant they were reluctant to admit that they might not be in control. Yet we are never in control.

Over time, the word uncertainty became normalised. We could no longer pretend that we were in control. Fear and polarisation were prevalent, the topic of mental health rose further on the agenda of organisations, and there was a recognition that uncertainty was here to stay, for quite a while at least. Clients realised they were leading through uncertainty and felt the emotional impact of it, yet they focused on creating more certainty by developing strategic vision, managing risk and building resilience for employees.

I've repeatedly watched clients try to exert control, only to discover that they get better results by softening their approach, letting go of attachment to a particular way and relaxing into their leadership. I witness them develop greater flexibility, adaptability and collaboration, leading to faster results. I believe our leadership is at its best when we allow it to be easy.

How this book is structured

This book is intended to provide new insights to the challenges we face of leading through uncertainty and the skills needed to create a new future. It encourages you to understand the emotional challenges that uncertainty invokes, and how you can overcome them through human connection.

In Part 1 of this book, I explore the context within which we are working today. I explain why I work with horses, how I came to work with them, the radical change we are experiencing in the world of work, the challenges we face as a human species in a technological world of fast-paced change, the need to evolve our leadership, and why compelling use of emotions is crucial for effective leadership.

Part 2 of the book explores the underlying emotional challenges we face when leading through uncertainty. I explain how uncertainty can lead to stress and overwhelm and how fear and polarisation are a fundamental part of navigating uncertainty.

Jude leading Opus (left) and Mr Blue (right)

I explore how past experiences, pain and trauma influence our default habits and behaviours. I also look at how we can lead more consciously and be more mindful of how we are triggered, and how that influences us and those around us. We cannot expect to resolve and eradicate emotional responses; instead we must include them in our leadership.

Part 3 of the book recommends that we return to the core of humanity and allow computers to do the fast processing, allowing us to slow down and be human. It explores some of the skills needed in uncertainty and how we can lead through our humanity rather than as robots. These skills can help leaders find more balance and be more resilient in navigating the emotional challenges we face when leading through uncertainty.

Each chapter opens with an illustrative horse story, key concepts are highlighted in boxed statements, and thought-provoking questions are accentuated in italics. Each chapter ends with pointers to master uncertainty, followed by questions aimed at provoking personal insight and self-reflection. Throughout the book, there are case studies from business leaders which provide examples of where more than one client has had the same or a similar experience. Names have been changed to protect client confidentiality. In some chapters, there are contributions from other industry leaders where appropriate.

Throughout this book I make reference to client experiences with the horses and what they learn, but mostly this is a book about uncertainty and leadership. For more information on how I work with horses, my first book, *Leadership Beyond Measure*, provides substantial background, theory and case studies, as well as my own learning from horses. Where I reference clients, I use examples that have been experienced by multiple people in the same way. I have also changed names to maintain anonymity. While the client case studies are true examples of what can happen, they reflect the experience of many people rather than one individual.

 Where you see this symbol, you will find reference to additional content, which is downloadable from my website at www.judejennison.com/uncertainty. This includes a workbook to capture your personal insights, white papers and other resources.

This book explains that however much you plan for every eventuality, nothing is certain in life, and we can lead in a new way without being reactive. I hope this book provokes reflection on your own leadership, as well as consideration for how you can support your team and organisation as you lead through uncertainty.

Are you ready for the ride?

Part 1

THE CONTEXT OF UNCERTAINTY

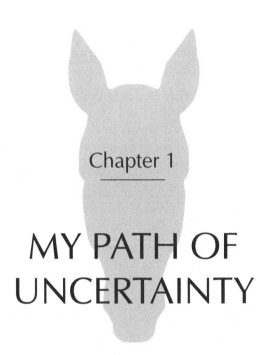

Chapter 1

MY PATH OF
UNCERTAINTY

"If you can lead a horse, you can lead anyone."

"That's a lot of horse!" I thought.

That was an understatement. Kalle was majestic. I watched her gallop up and down the arena. With her mane and tail flying behind her and her head held high, she snorted loudly as she charged from one end to the other. It was clear that she was strong, powerful and opinionated. I knew nothing about horses, but she certainly didn't look like a horse who was suitable for a novice such as me.

I had no reference point for this moment. I had only recently overcome my fear of horses. My previous experience had included six months riding at the age of nine and three serious accidents around horses as an adult, one while I was riding and two others on the ground. I write about these more

17

extensively in *Leadership Beyond Measure* so I won't go into them here. What I will say is that I was a novice, and I knew very little about horses. The only thing that was certain was that I was here to look at a horse to work with me. Despite Kalle charging up and down at an alarming rate, I walked calmly into the arena and stood in the middle. Having overcome my fear of horses only six months earlier, it seemed a brave thing to do. I'm not sure why I did it, but I followed my instincts and stepped into the arena of uncertainty. I felt as though my heart would stop, and I breathed deeply.

As soon as I walked in, Kalle came to a stop at the other end of the arena. I stayed calm, breathing consciously and grounding myself. She walked over to me and stood by my right shoulder. She looked me deep in the eye, and I felt the soul to soul connection that she creates so magically. I gulped and felt my eyes well up with tears. I was moved by the power and gentleness of her spirit. I walked forward, and Kalle came with me. I stopped, and she stopped with me. I paused, trying to breathe.

Kalle gallops at full speed

I moved again, turning left and right, stopping and starting. Kalle matched me step for step. When I moved, she came. When I stopped, she did, too. The connection felt so deep, yet I had no idea what I was doing. I had virtually no experience around horses. I had stepped right out of my depth and dived head first into the deep end of uncertainty.

I was completely unskilled in looking after a horse. I was uncertain whether she was suitable or if I could handle her. I could feel the power of her palpating beside me, and my heart was pounding. She was choosing to follow me as a leader, even though I had no idea what I was doing. I have received no greater acknowledgement of my leadership than in that moment. Kalle chose to follow with complete free will. It was and continues to be a deeply moving experience.

I went back to the gate to talk to her owner, Julie. Kalle was loose, but she stayed by my side as I went. I said to Julie, "She's so responsive. She's the kind of horse I could really connect with." At that moment, Kalle turned, looked me in the eye, and she nodded. My heart lurched, and I swallowed hard.

I was chosen.

What led me here?

In 2010, I left a 16-year career at IBM. After numerous senior leadership roles, including managing a European budget of $1 billion, I knew there was more for me in life. In hindsight, I was close to burnout, but I didn't realise it until I took a year's sabbatical and slowed down almost to a stop. After that sabbatical, I set up a leadership and coaching business with the desire to help senior leaders and executives work in harmony by finding their inner peace as well as creating outer peace. I knew what it was like to work in a large organisation, feeling ground down under the pressure of a heavy workload with aggressive targets to reach. I knew the stresses and strains of trying to work collaboratively in a high-pressure, high-performance culture with no let-up. I also knew how energising, exciting and rewarding it could be. The uncertainty that comes with a high-performance culture is immense. Stretch targets become the norm, and nobody knows whether they can meet them. It's an environment rife with uncertainty. Some people thrive on it, others are left reeling.

Having completed a year-long transformational leadership programme with The Coaches Training Institute, I also knew there was another way to lead, if only people had the skills to do so. Ironically, in the times when we are under pressure to succeed, there is a tendency to speed up, and in so doing we often lose our ability to lead effectively. What is needed in those moments is a slower, more grounded pace, a way of connecting to your authentic leadership and finding your flow with ease. Athletes know what it is like to be in the zone and spend years working with a performance coach to help them achieve it. Leaders who find this flow are not only powerful, compelling and engaging, they are often less stressed, more grounded and calmer. It makes good business sense to create an environment for leaders to thrive in this way. Yet in the current world of fast-paced change, everything is uncertain, and few people find the space to create that flow.

When I set up my leadership and coaching business in 2010, horses were not on my radar. By 2011, I was at a stud farm, completely out of my depth, choosing a horse.

Following my heart

When I left my corporate career, everyone said I was courageous, and some wished they could leave too. Why didn't they? Fear of uncertainty and fear of failure. The fear of uncertainty causes us to maintain the status quo, even if it isn't working. Leaving behind a highly paid career with all the financial benefits it brings to set up a small business in the middle of a recession is not for the faint-hearted! In hindsight, what others saw as courage was merely naivety, something I find serves me well in moments of uncertainty. If we overthink things, we don't move forward.

Although I had substantial experience working in a large global corporation of more than 400,000 employees worldwide, and I was comfortable managing a European budget of $1 billion, nothing could have prepared me for running a small business on my own. When I added horses into the mix, the uncertainty grew exponentially. Everything was unknown. I was on my own with no support structure, and the learning curve was fast. Failure was a definite possibility. Over the coming months and years, I would fail repeatedly, pick myself up and try again. Had I known that, I might have stayed in my corporate career. We have a psychological need for safety and tend to seek it naturally. Uncertainty is a threat to our safety, yet it is unavoidable if we want to create breakthroughs.

One of the first leadership programmes I ran was a six-month programme for a group of IT directors. It was called "Challenge the status quo" and was designed to help them increase self-awareness and be more bold and courageous in their leadership. In between workshops, I gave them practical challenges to develop their leadership further, one of which was to overcome their fear of something. I'm a great believer in walking my talk and won't ask anyone to do anything I wouldn't be willing to do myself. And so I found myself working with someone to help me overcome my fear of horses. Despite my fear, I kept being drawn to horses without knowing why. I had no intention of riding again, so my decision to overcome my fear of them was to put the fear to rest and move on.

Little did I know what was in store. I overcame my fear of horses in the first five minutes of being in their presence and learned so much about my own leadership in the first two hours. I talk about this experience in more detail in *Leadership Beyond Measure*. Suffice to say here that I discovered Equine Guided Leadership, which is a way of working with horses to develop leadership and communication skills.

21

Following that first session, instead of putting my fascination with horses to rest, it reignited it, and I found myself drawn to learning more about working with them. Still with no intention of doing the work, I embarked on an extensive training programme to train as a HorseDream Partner, an international methodology designed to work specifically with corporate leaders and teams.

Uncertainty was at play in abundance.

Throughout the training, I found myself working with people who had their own horses and were very confident and competent around them. I was unsure why I was doing the training, but I followed my instincts and trusted that I was meant to be there. I was willing to explore and see what happened. The only thing that was certain was that it felt right. In moments of uncertainty, we tend to rely on logic and reasoning, yet our instincts are rarely wrong. Effective leaders trust their intuition in uncertainty and include it in the decision-making process.

I had no desire to ride horses, yet there was also no doubt that I was in the right place. In only eight months, I overcame my fear, attended intensive training, qualified as a HorseDream Partner, delivered my first corporate workshop and took ownership of my first horse.

Life was moving fast, and I was galloping along the path of uncertainty with no idea where I was heading.

Facing uncertainty head on

After seeing Kalle charging up and down the arena, I knew deep down that she was the right horse for me. My heart was sure, my gut instinct was clear, but my head was questioning the sanity of taking on such a majestic animal when my capabilities of handling horses were virtually non-existent. I didn't even know how to put on a head collar.

I went home to think about it. I wanted to be sure I was doing the right thing. In moments of uncertainty, we look for certainty, glimpses that we are on the right track. Things were moving fast, and I felt the need to slow down the decision and give myself time to pause for breath. Kalle is 16.2 hands high (which is 1.68m to the top of the shoulder), bigger than I had intended as a first horse. She is a German breed called Trakehner, known for being spirited and highly sensitive. Riders often say this breed is tricky to handle. Knowing nothing about horses, I was oblivious to this. I discovered that they are highly sensitive and intuitive, making them perfect for my work.

I had limited experience around horses, and this was a huge decision. At the time, many people said I was bold. Others told me I was crazy. I didn't see it in either of those ways. When people questioned my capability, I replied that nobody knows how to look after a child until they have one – you just have to learn. And fast! I followed my heart and knew that this was the work I wanted to do. Exactly eight months after I overcame my fear of horses, Kalle came into my life. Clients had been asking to work with horses, so I decided I'd better get a horse!

If I had any doubts about taking on a horse as powerful as Kalle, I was certain my friends would not let me play small. Later that day, I spoke to a dear friend, Nicole, and explained that Kalle was big, powerful, spirited, kind and gentle and that I was a little concerned that she might be too much for clients. Nicole asked whether I could handle her. I replied that I thought so. To which Nicole responded, "If you think you can handle her and your clients can't, then you are holding your clients too small." With that I made the decision. I took ownership of Kalle one month later.

My path of uncertainty had most definitely begun.

Chapter 2

HUMAN BEINGS VS SUPERCOMPUTERS

"When you reach your limit, stop, reflect and find another way. The challenge is to know when your limit has been reached."

"Sit down and be quiet."

The words of my childhood years at school. I was told what to do, how to do it, and I was expected to follow the instructions. I was rewarded when I did and reprimanded when I fell short. Things were fairly black and white. Pretty certain. The world looks very different today.

Now you are competing against technology for your job. You're not a robot, but you often feel like one.

You are expected to be creative and innovative, but must not fail or make mistakes. You are encouraged to be empowered and take responsibility, but there are five levels of signoff to buy printer paper. You are told what to do and how to do it, but criticised for not being agile and decisive. You have to meet tight deadlines and stretch targets, but there are insufficient people to do the work.

As a result, you've been given enough workload for three people but are not considered resilient enough when you get stressed.

The hierarchy is flattening, so you now have more than one boss, and they have different ideas about your priorities and objectives.

I hope you are superhuman.

Rapid pace of change

Have you ever wished there were more hours in the day? Do you find yourself permanently rushing from one place to another? Do you get to the end of the day only to discover you haven't achieved the things you planned to do?

We live in extraordinary times. Life and work are changing at an alarming pace in ways we cannot predict, and at times it leaves people feeling exposed, uneasy and uncomfortable. People are increasingly connected to technology and disconnected at an emotional and physical level. It's not unusual to see a family of four at a restaurant all on their mobile phones, physically present but with their attention elsewhere.

Technology processes high volumes of data, and the human brain is unable to match the computer in processing power. As such, our view of the pace and volume of data that we can process is skewed. The rapid advancement of technology has fuelled a high pace of change and has led to constant bombardment of information or "noise", making it harder for people to switch off.

Fast-paced change and increasing amounts of information in organisations create overwhelm, a jumbled mind and "head spin", where people grasp for the answers and information amongst a plethora of data. Some cope with this by tuning out external distractions, focusing on their own needs and disconnecting from those around them. Others engage and vie for attention and their opinion to be accepted as the "right answer". The perceived connection is not real but self-driven from the ego.

Who are you disconnected from?

We are not machines and the ever-increasing pace is not sustainable for human beings. We are bombarded by information, but we cannot process it at the same pace as a computer does. As computer processing power increases in speed, our view of what is possible becomes further skewed, and people put themselves under increased pressure to try to keep up. The uncertainty of operating in an environment like this is immense, and the continuous uncertainty and pressure can lead to overwhelm and overload. There is no headspace for reflection, and people find themselves caught up in the swell.

Organisations measure numerical results and financial targets rather than relationships, collaboration and innovation, leading to further disconnection as people work towards competing objectives. The volume of information available exacerbates the desire to achieve aggressive targets and drives a high-performance culture. While organisations continue to make financial targets more important than engagement and human connection, leaders will continually strive for individual rather than collective success.

Working in this way can lead to burnout and mental health issues. When the pressure is on to deliver, human connection is one of the first things to suffer. We have to find another way to use technology instead of being used by it. Business results are now generated by a combination of people and technology. We provide the right environment for technology to work. We need to afford people the environment where they can thrive, too. That is human connection.

Human beings vs supercomputers

Human beings process information in a contextual way, which includes the environment, emotions and systems around us. We get distracted by information because we emotionally engage with it, whereas computers do not.

> *If we establish that we are not superhuman and not machines, who are we? What is the core of humanity?*

If we use computers and robots to do the work that we can't do, we can focus on the core of what makes us human, which is creativity and thought leadership, embracing the skills of nurturing, community and connection. We can do that without burning out and having a nervous breakdown. Computers, by contrast, can process high volumes of data, sort it logically and provide output that enables us to make decisions effectively.

We compete with computers for speed and volume. It's a competition we cannot win. Computers don't have a finite capacity because we upgrade them and expand their capacity whereas the human capacity for processing is finite. If your phone fills up with photos, you either delete information or upgrade the phone to hold more. You cannot currently upgrade your brain to process information faster. I hope you never will. As human beings, we have expanded our capabilities for decades in parallel to the processing power of computers. We need to recognise that we have our limits when it comes to processing information and that we need to operate within them. We must ensure we retain the core of our humanity and work alongside technology without needing to become it.

We need to consider the capabilities of humanity. It's not processing 500 emails a day with 50 WhatsApp messages and all the social media platforms spewing out misinformation. We can't physically, mentally and emotionally process everything, and we should not try to do so.

We have trained our brains to operate at high speed and don't know how to switch off. We are more overstimulated than ever before, and our brains are constantly whirring, leading to stress and overwhelm. As technology evolves, we are unconsciously making the assumption that we can evolve at the same pace of processing. All of this exacerbates the uncertainty.

Where are you running at full speed and need to slow down?

Gio and Mr Blue chase each other in the snow

In the Industrial Age, we created machines that were operated by us to speed up our ability to do our work. Now our work is determined by technology. Technology drives the pace of work and change, and we cannot control the quality and volume of information that exists in the world today. Either we respond to technological advances, or we become obsolete in the market place. Technology-based businesses such as Amazon, Uber and Airbnb disrupt the way we live and work, and that creates uncertainty for legacy businesses which need to adapt quickly to survive. Those who lack the agility to adapt quickly and to be flexible could lose their jobs or their businesses. Uncertainty and the rapidly changing world work for those who are early adopters and fast to respond. If you are in this camp, it's easier, but for many of your team, it may be much harder to embrace change. We need to help people adapt to this new way of behaving.

Data and information drive our behaviour. Smartphones, tablets and nanotechnology tell us what to eat, when to move, how to meditate and so on. We can't go back to how things were, but we can choose how we use technology and how it drives our decisions now and in the future. Most importantly, we can choose how it affects humanity. But will we?

The ethics of technology

Technology raises questions of ethics to consider and address. The rise of artificial intelligence has major implications for the future of work, business, employees, society and the human race.

While technology has enabled substantial progress through research and faster processing, it affects our security, privacy and society. It becomes increasingly difficult to opt out of technological advances that erode privacy, like the apps that tell you where the airport check-in desk is because it knows you've arrived and also knows which airline you are travelling on. It is likely that future generations will not have a concept of privacy in the way we do today. Is that a good or a bad thing? However you view it, the consequences of how we choose to use technology influence our everyday behaviour, and this increases the uncertainty with which we live and work.

The Deloitte Global Human Capital Trends report 2017[1] indicates that the pace of change of technology is growing

---

[1] B. Walsh and E. Volini, Rewriting the rules for the digital age, Deloitte Global Human Capital Trends (2017). Available from: www2.deloitte.com/content/dam/Deloitte/global/Documents/About-Deloitte/central-europe/ce-global-human-capital-trends.pdf [accessed 18 March 2018].

exponentially, followed by people, business and lastly public bodies. Government organisations and public bodies are slow to respond to the impact of technological change. When new technology is released, nobody can be sure what will be widely adopted and how it might influence how we live and work. If technology businesses are influencing our future, and if government organisations and public bodies are not providing the guidelines, who will?

We have the opportunity to assess the impact of what we are doing with technology before it is too late. But will we? And are we moving fast enough?

The vast changes in business and society create uncertainty for all of us in both our working and personal lives. It is possible to use technology as a force for good, to create opportunities and enhance society, but it relies on the few who make those decisions to consider the impact from all angles. Given that people are incentivised by targets and not by the impact on humanity, there is no guarantee that all decisions will be ethical and life-enhancing for all. We can change that. It is the responsibility of every leader to ensure that the decisions we make *are* enhancing and *do* benefit society in the longer term. It's not acceptable for leaders to line their own pockets with bonuses and pay rises without considering the enormous impact we have as leaders, and the responsibility we take on for shaping the future of our world.

Our decisions create an impact, consciously or unconsciously. It is the responsibility of all business leaders to act wisely and consciously to create a sustainable future that is life-enhancing for all.

What decisions are you making today that will affect the future for generations to come?

Artificial intelligence is growing in sophistication, and the current expectation is that 30% of all jobs will be performed by artificial intelligence by 2030. Whether this becomes a reality or not, the role of the employee will continue to change as information and data processing will be performed by computers far faster and more efficiently than humans ever could manage it. This raises an interesting question over what we value in business and how we reward people. How do we reconcile the fact that care workers, nurses and social workers, whose work cannot be automated, are paid so little compared with lawyers and accountants whose work could be automated in the future?

How do we redress the balance of pay so that we reward emotional intelligence, social responsibility, compassion and caring for the community as well as intellect?

How do we create a world where humanity is as important as information and knowledge when the latter can be mechanised and the former cannot?

The uncertainty of our time is being driven by the increased adoption of technology and has wide-reaching implications for all of us. This is not new, of course. In the Industrial Age, human action was replaced by machines, but the pace of change is accelerating, and therefore the uncertainty is increasing, and that has an emotional impact. We can use technology to improve the way we live and work if we make decisions consciously, but the ethical debate around technology needs to be considered by all of us.

How can you use technology more consciously and recognise the impact it has on your daily life?

Connection or disconnection?

People use technology as a way of disconnecting from things that feel uncomfortable, such as standing in a queue in a coffee shop, or waiting for a train, bus or taxi. Even in meetings, when things get uncomfortable people distract themselves from the moment by using technology to disconnect from the emotion as well as from those around them.

> *We use technology to disconnect when the connection or the learning is uncomfortable. It acts as a comfort blanket, something we can rely on to make us feel better in uncomfortable situations.*

You hear stories of people being fired by text message. How cruel is that? The person sending the text avoids seeing and feeling the emotional pain of the person on the receiving end. How sad that we feel the need to disconnect emotionally from one another and cannot be with each other's pain. It's essential for leaders to develop their emotional capacity to feel their own feelings and lead through and with them, as well as empathising with others and supporting them through their process.

As a species, we are more connected and also more disconnected than ever before. Families are widely dispersed globally. As children growing up, we were in and out of each other's homes, sharing the laughter, the joy, the pain and sadness, too. Emotion was a fundamental part of our lives. Connection was obvious and effortless, and our sphere of connection and community was local.

In the backdrop of human to human disconnection, the desire for connection has not gone away as it is a fundamental part of being human. Instead, people seek connection via social media, finding people they agree with, who share their ideas and opinions, shutting down from anyone who may be different. As the world of business seeks to embrace more diverse opinions, the way we use technology creates the opposite approach. Online search engines have been programmed to decide what you see on your news feed, based on past searches and what you have liked. Technology influences what you do and don't see, and that impacts your opinions and beliefs.

Although people bare their soul on social media, there is a sense of disconnection from the heart, from community and from family. We have an opportunity to use technology to connect rather than disconnect, and we need the emotional resilience to allow us to be with the differences that world views bring.

Collaboration not competition

There is a need to work in collaboration with technology rather than competing with it on pace and output. We are no longer bound by our immediate local community in life and work. Technology can expand your horizons and that increases the uncertainty. The limitless opportunities for connection and collaboration can be overwhelming, so the tendency can be to shut it down. In addition, the facelessness of technology can lead to disconnection. We cannot see someone's emotional response when we send an email, text or WhatsApp message. While emoticons give you some idea of the sender's emotion, using technology has become a way of avoiding the emotional impact of empathy. Instead of giving bad news face to face, people have taken the cowardly way out of communicating via technology. Technology used in this way creates emotional disconnection, which has a major impact on our society.

> *We need a more conscious awareness of how we use technology going forward to ensure we develop it and use it to enhance business and society.*

Technology has had a hugely positive impact on how we live and work, advancing solutions in healthcare, renewable energy and business in general. It enables us to collaborate globally on projects that we previously could not, expanding the realms of what is possible and embracing different cultures and ways of working.

While research can be performed faster with technology, there is a genuine concern about the quality of the data on the internet. The rise of social media has brought about popular commentary where anyone can share their opinion as if it were a fact, and much of it is very convincing. Where previously people referred to specific journalists for facts and information, the internet is now awash with supposed scientific reports that contradict each other. We no longer know what to believe and this can cause people to be misguided or, worse, disengaged through overwhelm. Leaders need to focus and gain clarity on what to pay attention to and what to ignore. The ability to sift out important information is critical to how decisions are made.

Successful leaders in the future will integrate technological advances with their innate wisdom and emotions to ensure we create a future of connection rather than disconnection.

MASTERING UNCERTAINTY

- Notice where technology skews your thinking on what is humanly possible.

- Be aware that you and your team cannot match technology in the speed and volume of data processing.

- Consider the ethics of how you use technology and the impact it has on individuals, business and society.

- Use technology to create connection across borders and cultures.

- Pay attention to where technology creates disconnection, both emotionally and physically.

- Use technology responsibly and ethically to enhance human experience in society.

Before you move on to the next chapter, spend 10 minutes reflecting on how technology affects your behaviour.

 Download the *Leading Through Uncertainty* workbook from www.judejennison.com/uncertainty and record your reflections.

PROVOKING PERSONAL INSIGHT

Who are you disconnected from?

Where are you running at full speed and need to slow down?

What decisions are you making today that will affect the future for generations to come?

How can you use technology more consciously and recognise the impact it has on your daily life?

Chapter 3

EMOTIONAL ENGAGEMENT

"Self-awareness, self-confidence and self-belief are foundations for leading through uncertainty."

"Pick me," the horse seemed to be saying.

I had gone to see a horse called Gio, and my eyes were drawn to the large black horse in the stable at the end. His eyes locked onto mine, and I hoped it would be him. The yard owner, Julie, led me down the yard and indeed, the beautiful black horse was Gio. I entered his stable. His heart was racing with anxiety, and he was trying to hold it all together. I wasn't sure he was suitable to work with me and my clients. I didn't want an anxious horse. My horses need to be confident in their own skin because clients are often anxious when they arrive.

I looked Gio in the eye and felt the depth of his connection as he drew me in. My heart desperately wanted to say yes, I'll take him, but my head overruled my emotion because I couldn't risk taking on an anxious horse. I already had a horse called Tiffin, who gets overwhelmed with anxious clients. It was too big a risk. All logic and reasoning made it clear that Gio was not the horse for me.

Meanwhile, my heart was telling me a different story. In the course of my work, I often help leaders reduce their anxiety and find a place of greater calm in uncertainty. I wanted to help Gio find his new home so he could relax and be less anxious, and I found myself committing to him that I would help him. It felt like a crazy thing to do to tell a horse I would help him find the right home. I had no idea how I might do that, and I didn't exactly have the time to keep going to visit him either. But somehow it felt the right thing to do. There was something about him that kept me going back.

Each time I returned, Gio was pleased to see me. On one occasion, he was out in the field, and nobody had been able to get near him with a head collar. We thought he had become semi-feral since being out in the field with no human interaction. I went out with a head collar, thinking if the experienced grooms could not get near him, there was no way I would, as a novice horse owner.

I approached the gate of the field where he was grazing with three other horses. As I walked through the gate, he looked up and trotted over to me. Clearly he recognised me. I put the head collar over his head, convinced he wouldn't leave without the other horses. Horses are herd animals and find their safety with other horses, so sometimes a young horse will not go on their own. He walked with me without faltering. He had decided I was his new owner, and he would not go with anyone else!

Horses are highly sensitive creatures, as people are. The uncertainty about Gio's future made him anxious. He seemed to know that I was willing to help him, and he became less anxious as a result. I decided I would take a risk with him after all. In hindsight, I was Gio's last chance at life, and he seemed to know it, too.

I'd integrated the wisdom of my head, heart and gut and found the ideal solution for both of us. Gio has turned out to be amazing at working with clients. He's huge at 17.2 hands tall (approx. 1.78m to the top of his shoulder), but extremely gentle. He seems to recognise that he could trample us and is extraordinarily sensitive and respectful around people. I liken it to being a human being not wanting to step on a cat! Gio is a natural connector, wanting to be with people and yearning for a job. Since settling into his new life with me, he has a purpose for the first time in his seven years, and his anxiety has reduced as his life has become more certain. Uncertainty creates anxiety in other species, not just humans.

Thinking and feeling

Gio's anxiety over the uncertainty of his future almost prevented me from taking him on. His emotions almost derailed his opportunity for a new role working with me. That's the challenge of leading through uncertainty. Uncertainty puts everyone under pressure, and emotions become more difficult to manage under pressure. This is the crux of the challenge we face in business today. We cannot pretend emotions don't exist because they are a fundamental part of what it is to be human. Uncertainty magnifies them.

My rational brain had decided Gio was not suitable as he lacked confidence. It was only when I was willing to look beyond this and try to make sense of him and his emotions that I was able to recognise that he had potential and could grow in confidence. As I created more certainty for him, his anxiety reduced, his confidence increased, and I realised that he was in fact perfect to work with me and my clients.

We have historically made logical reasoning more important than emotions. The most effective leaders integrate the two. Most people have done psychological assessments and used personality profiling tools that identify habits and behaviours. The either/or approach puts people in boxes and labels their behaviour. While it is a useful to create a starting point of self-awareness, people sometimes use labels as an excuse for behaviour and get stuck in a loop of doing things a particular way. Our personality is not permanently fixed. We can learn to expand upon our default habits and behaviours and in so doing develop our leadership.

We are emotional and intellectual beings. We have the capacity to both think and feel, and we are at our most effective when we bridge the gap between the two. Most people have developed the muscle of one over the other, yet truly effective decisions integrate both critical thinking and emotional feelings.

Horses invite us to integrate. If we fail to think through what we want from them, the lack of clarity makes it unsafe for them to follow. Equally, unless we establish an emotional connection, they refuse to come with us. The absence of emotion is incongruent and makes horses feel unsafe. People will come based on rank and authority, but in those moments you are not leading, and the cooperation is not sustainable. Horses provide feedback on how integrated our leadership is. They need clarity through rational thought, integrated with emotional connection. So do your team. While your team may come with you because of a hierarchy, horses make it clear when your leadership is fully integrated, following you when it is and refusing to move when it is not.

Are your team cooperating because they have to or because they want to?

The power of thought provides us with the capability to analyse data and information and make sense of it. This is something that computers and robots can be programmed to do. Computers can process data far quicker than human beings can, and we have the potential to use them to alleviate the stress and workload for the human race.

However, at the moment, robots cannot feel. Our emotional response is at the heart of what it is to be human – the desire to take care of one another, to build community, to nurture and support, to fall in and out of love. All of these human experiences are driven by your emotional responses – your feelings. Feelings create uncertainty too as they cannot always be rationalised. We've learned to shut them down in business and replace them with the drive for results. With the increased uncertainty at work, emotions run high under the surface, regardless of whether we acknowledge them. We need to redress the balance and integrate both thinking and feeling so that we can make decisions wisely and effectively.

Emotional judgement

Many people I work with say that their biggest challenge is getting people to do what they need them to do. Often they use logic and reasoning to persuade and influence. Conversely, people engage emotionally. Effective use of emotions therefore can encourage connection and cooperation.

Emotions are part of the human experience. When we meet someone for the first time, we instantly make an emotional decision about them. We decide whether we trust them or not, whether they are credible or not, whether they are good at their job or not. We make instant decisions with a handshake. We can change that decision, but once an opinion has been formed emotionally, we use logic and reasoning later to justify our initial judgement.

If you feel an instant dislike for someone on first meeting, or you think they are not credible, it's typically a decision based on emotions or gut instinct. Everything you see in the next days, week, months and years will be logical reasoning and facts that back up the decision you made at the first handshake. Your brain will ignore the information that proves the opposite unless the information is very compelling. We may think we make decisions rationally in business, but emotions unconsciously have a huge influence. That's why it's important to develop our awareness of how we use our emotions, especially in uncertainty when they become more apparent. I had made an emotional attachment to Gio in that first meeting, an attachment that saved his life and provided me with an incredible horse to work with.

Emotions have a huge influence on our behaviour. When people walk through the gate to meet me and the horses for the first time, they experience a range of emotional responses. Some people are excited, and some people are eager to get stuck in because they love a challenge and love being out of their comfort zone. These are the people who thrive on uncertainty.

Many more people are extremely uncomfortable being out of their comfort zone and need support and guidance to help them feel more secure. They may respond by shutting down, reflecting, sitting back and observing. Often the masks come up and they hold back. People behave in a way they feel that they should rather than as who they really are. Some people say, "I don't see the point of this. I don't want to do it. It's a waste of my time. It's ridiculous." These people are so far out of their comfort zone and so uneasy with something new and different that they want to shut it down and make it wrong. The situation may be too uncomfortable so they ridicule it. As people start to feel more within their comfort zone, they begin to relax, are more willing to engage and become more effective. When you understand why people behave in a particular way, you cease to take it personally and can work with them instead.

The more comfortable you are leading out of your comfort zone, the more able you are to deal with uncertainty. Developing confidence in dealing with the unknown is a crucial part of leading through uncertainty. Knowing where your comfort zone is helps you continually expand your leadership capabilities.

A client and Gio work together out of their comfort zones

Organisations have a range of people, from those who thrive on a challenge to those who resist change and refuse to do anything new, and those in the middle who are trying hard to adapt but get stressed in the process. The group in the middle will flip in and out of being willing and resistant. They may push through their resistance to get results, but may get overwhelmed in the process. When you recognise who in your team is comfortable with uncertainty and who is not, you can support people better.

When we operate repeatedly out of our comfort zone without time and space to reflect and recharge, we get stressed and over-whelmed. When you develop self-awareness and have confidence in your leadership, you can develop the knowledge that even when you feel unskilled, you are still capable of leading effectively. You can reduce the stress of uncertainty by increasing self-confidence and self-belief, as well as by becoming more comfortable with not knowing the answers.

What can you count on yourself for in uncertainty?

What do you know that is true about you no matter what happens – whether you are the CEO of a global bank or home-less in the street?

Our identity is caught up in the roles that we play. If I do a good job, there is an implication that it makes me a good person. If I'm made redundant, I am somehow less of a person, less worthy, but we are not the roles that we play and the jobs that we do.

> *We are rewarded on what we do, who we are and how we show up, but the integrity of our humanity doesn't change with how well we do our job. The world is changing and people need more than results and numbers. Results and numbers benefit only a select few. Purpose, meaning, connection to self and humanity have enormous value, too.*

Suppressing emotions

When things are uncertain, emotions run high. To squash emotions and pretend they don't exist denies us the full human experience and ignores the wisdom that guides effective decision-making. Ignoring your emotions increases stress and leads to overwhelm. When we make emotions wrong in business, we hold that it's not ok to be angry or scared or anxious because it's "unprofessional". All those emotions we have as part of the natural human experience are shut down because we've deemed them to be inappropriate in the workplace.

> *Emotions have been made wrong in business because people use them in an unskilled way. The unskilled usage of emotions comes from a lack of practice.*

If you regularly stifle your emotions and don't allow yourself to express them in the moment, your emotions will explode at an inappropriate moment in a less professional way. We've probably all experienced explosions of emotion in the office. When horses suppress their emotions, they become unpredictable and explosive, and that makes them dangerous. We all have moments of unskilled behaviour with emotions as most people have not been trained to use them in a powerful way throughout their life. From as early as being a toddler, you learn that it's not appropriate to have a tantrum in the middle of a supermarket just because you can't have your own way. In the process, we learn to adopt a new behaviour – that of withholding emotion, which leads to the ultimate explosion at an untimely moment.

Anger builds up when we suppress frustration over a period of time and pretend it's not happening. When your emotion says "I'm feeling frustrated", it's just information. Be curious. Why are you frustrated? Frustration indicates unmet needs and desires. Instead of being frustrated and letting it build out of proportion, ask for what you want. The frustration can guide you more powerfully to make effective decisions and meet your needs if you are curious about it as a source of information instead of suppressing it.

Anger often comes from unresolved frustration that has been suppressed repeatedly over time. The quicker you resolve minor frustrations and disagreements, the less likely it is that they will grow out of proportion and out of control. Your emotions tell you what wants to happen.

What emotion are you suppressing and what impact is that having?

Uncertainty increases our emotions. The self-awareness required to manage your emotions grows exponentially alongside the volume of pressure that you are subjected to. The more pressure you feel, the harder it is to manage your emotions. That's why it's important to create a culture where people feel comfortable expressing their needs so that there is no need to resort to unskilled explosions.

> *Emotion is a way of expressing a desire that is met or unmet. If you allow yourself to feel the emotion and become curious about it, you can use it as a source of wisdom to understand what you want to create.*

Organisations are full of people who are disengaged. Yes, they work hard, yes they are driven, yes they deliver. But why?

Many people I meet love their job and may love their business but feel under excessive pressure to perform. They are driven by fear of failure or fear of getting it wrong, fear of not being good enough, missing out on the next promotion or being made redundant. Yet they are afraid to be explicit about this level of pressure for fear of the consequences.

Are your team coming with you through fear or because they are engaged?

How do you know?

One is leadership, the other is not. While people may be driven by fear, horses will not. They will refuse to cooperate until you engage them through relationship, clarity and a sense of purpose.

The future of business depends on creating a culture where people can be truly human. If you overlook the humanity and strive only for results and financial returns, people eventually lose focus and disengage. Emotions are therefore critical to the engagement of your team.

Case study – client team

The team had pushed themselves so far beyond their limits that they were exhausted. As soon as they walked through the gate, the horses all lay down in the field. I asked the clients how they felt. Initially they all said they were fine. It was a standard response. They were used to coping and carrying on.

Eventually, one of them admitted to being "a bit tired". Once one person opened up, the others all admitted that they were under significant pressure and exhausted. Once they had named it, the horses stood up again.

The clients had put themselves under repeated pressure to perform to the point where they were exhausted. Nobody wanted to admit it because they had subconsciously believed it was a weakness. Many people continue to put themselves under incessant pressure without taking time to recharge or to recognise their emotions, and this is taking its toll in organisations with the rise of mental health issues.

Source of wisdom

Many of the people I work with, from executive boards to graduates and leaders at all levels in between, have suppressed their emotions so much that they do not possess language to describe how they feel in different situations.

One of the first things I ask clients to do when they work with horses is to observe them and name the primary emotion they experience watching the horses. Often people say they feel intrigued or curious. These are cognitive responses, seeking information and facts. When pushed to describe their emotions, people are often uncomfortable. It's unusual for them to admit they feel scared, overwhelmed or anxious about doing something they've not done before. They would hardly ever dare to be that transparent in the office, and they lack the language to describe how they feel.

Yet as soon as people name how they feel, the stress begins to reduce and the group become more supportive of each other, recognising that they all feel vulnerable in some way. Once expressed, the emotion no longer has a hold over them. Instead, they can use it as a source of information and consider how they proceed. Those who are terrified may want to hold back and watch others first. I offer to help people reduce their fear, and most willingly accept. The fear of not wanting to feel an emotion can cause a lack of productivity and lead to not addressing the emotion itself and therefore not meeting your needs. If you don't create the space to feel your emotions, you can't move on because you don't have space to process it and take meaning from it.

> *Emotions are released by deepening our experience of them, making sense of them and then letting them go. When you give yourself permission to feel, you realise that feelings don't take over – you can have an emotion without losing control and without the emotion taking over.*

When we are transparent about our emotions, we can create what we want, knowing it is informed by a deep desire, not just a cognitive process. When you get stuck in the loop of a negative emotion or an unmet need, it can feel as though it is taking over, but it doesn't need to be squashed either. There is a way of balancing emotions and using them as a powerful source of information. High-performing teams talk transparently about their emotions and create space to vent their emotions when things get tough, as they often do. They provide support to help each other recover more quickly. They know that unresolved emotions have an impact and need to be cleared to move forward.

Emotions last only a minute and a half. Imagine that. Most of us get stuck in emotions for days on end. If you feel an emotion for longer than a minute and a half, it's because you are going round and round a situation and allowing yourself to get stuck in a loop of the emotion. Being honest about it can help release the hold it has on you and is an effective use of emotions to express the unmet need or desire.

Are you having emotions, or are your emotions having you?

The former is powerful use of emotions and can guide you to make powerful decisions based on a deeper embodied wisdom. The latter is where the emotion takes over and you reach an unpowerful state. Increasing self-awareness enables you to notice the habits and behaviours you exhibit and the emotions that drive your behaviour. You can fully integrate the head, heart and gut when you pay attention to your whole body experience.

When leaders believe that all of their problems lie externally, they do not take responsibility for their emotions and do not change their behaviour. Therefore, the challenges they face continue. One client explained to me that he found everyone difficult to deal with. He expected them to conform to his view of the way things should be done, and when they did not, he engaged in conflict with them. He was unaware that he had a role to play in influencing others by changing his own behaviour first.

We evoke change in others when we take responsibility for our emotions, actions and behaviours. This in itself requires a self-awareness to explore what we do, how we do it and the impact it has on others.

Change happens when we willingly accept the impact of our behaviour and how emotions influence it. Self-knowledge is the starting point, but our impact on others also influences their behaviour and has vital consequences.

MASTERING UNCERTAINTY

- Integrate rational thought, emotions and intuition in your decision-making. Don't just rely on logic and facts.

- Notice your initial emotional response to people and situations and be willing to alter your view by being open and curious.

- Take time to recharge when you are under pressure and encourage your team to recharge and recover as well.

- Notice where you suppress your emotions or where others withhold emotions.

- Allow yourself to feel an emotion, process it and use it as a source of information.

- Take responsibility for your emotions.

- Find ways to engage people emotionally in their work.

Before you move on to the next chapter, spend 10 minutes reflecting on how emotions drive your behaviour and that of your team.

 Download the *Leading Through Uncertainty* workbook from www.judejennison.com/uncertainty and record your reflections.

PROVOKING PERSONAL INSIGHT

Are your team cooperating because they have to or because they want to?

What can you count on yourself for in uncertainty?

What do you know that is true about you no matter what happens – whether you are the CEO of a global bank or homeless in the street?

What emotion are you suppressing and what impact is that having?

Are your team coming with you through fear or because they are engaged? How do you know?

Are you having emotions, or are your emotions having you?

Part 2
YOU ARE NOT A MACHINE!

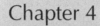

Chapter 4

STRESS AND
OVERWHELM

*"The current situation of faster technological
processing power fuelling more human workload is
not sustainable."*

Lying face down in a muddy pool of six inch deep water, my head was spinning and pounding. I heard the sound of someone hammering in the distance.

"Can you hear that banging?" I asked my husband, Paul, who stood beside me. "Is someone building a house?"

"No, I can't hear anything," he replied.

"I think I'm concussed," I said.

"Don't be silly," Paul said, as he held out his hand and helped me get to my feet.

I had asked Paul for help as I was struggling to get Kalle in and out of the field. The livery yard where she was kept had moved her to a new field where the gateway was made out of electric fence tape and the ground was waterlogged and deep in muddy water. The only way in and out of the field was to open the live electric gate in one hand, lead Kalle through with the other hand, turn round and hook the gate closed again. When the electric tape touched the wet ground, it sparked with a loud crack, causing Kalle to jump back in fear.

When you know what you are doing, it's a relatively simple manoeuvre to execute, but I was new to this. Everything was uncertain. I had to navigate a pool of muddy water, two metres wide by two metres long, leading a horse with one hand and holding sparking electric tape in the other. The potential risk to our safety was high. In fact, Kalle had already electrocuted us both only a couple of weeks earlier by touching the electric fence while I was leading her. She had reared up and left me shaking in fear. I was doing my utmost not to repeat the experience.

Kalle had repeatedly refused to walk through the gate in the last two days, and I had been unable to get her out of the field. I had a workshop with clients the next day, and I had no idea if I could get her out to work. I had asked the yard owner if we could switch off the electrics temporarily to help me, and she had refused, saying the other horses might escape. Unsure where else to turn, I asked my husband to come and hold the gate open so I could focus on leading Kalle through the muddy water. I thought that without the distraction of holding a sparking electric fence gate in the other hand, I might have a bit more success.

It had not gone according to plan. My lack of horsemanship skills was evident, and my leadership skills were lacking, too. I had tried to persuade Kalle to walk through the water, but she was very reluctant. Finally, after much persuasion, she agreed to follow me and started to walk through. I thought we had cracked it. At that moment, I slipped in the mud, and I felt myself falling face down into a pool of brown, murky water. In my unskilled way of leading a horse, I held onto Kalle's lead rope, trying to regain my balance. In doing so, I nearly brought 600 kg of horse down on top of me.

Kalle headbutted me out of the way, causing me to drop the lead rope, then she jumped over me to avoid crushing me. I knew in that moment she had done it to save me from serious injury. By contrast, the yard manager told me moments later that Kalle was naughty, badly behaved, had no manners and that I should have slapped her for headbutting me. She'd been watching at a distance with no offer of support.

I had to admit defeat. I could not look after a horse without adequate support. I am not superhuman. I am not a machine that can be programmed to do things a particular way, and neither is my horse. I was unskilled and leading through uncertainty with no support. I needed help. Fast. My life and my work depended on it.

Asking for help

Uncertainty and not knowing create stress. They are part of the process of change, innovation and creativity. As the levels of uncertainty in business and throughout the world are amplified, and as innovation and change generate more uncertainty, so too the level of stress in the workplace increases. There is no quick fix for this, and it is not going to disappear. We cannot expect to navigate our current life and working environments without stress. Instead, we need to learn to find ways to support ourselves and each other to navigate challenging situations without reaching a point of burnout and overwhelm.

I've spent my life doing what seems ordinary to me and extraordinary to others. I work at a fast pace, achieve high volumes of output in a short space of time and do things that everyone tells me are not possible. I like a challenge. I'm determined and motivated. I persevere when others give up. But I also have my limits.

In the moment that I was face down in mud with mild concussion, I had to admit I had reached them.

With little horse knowledge, a 600 kg powerful and opinionated horse on a yard where all I received was criticism, I knew I needed the right kind of support instead of the continuous blame and judgement for not doing things their way. I had repeatedly been open to listening to their advice and working together, but I drew the line at slapping my horse. My way was clearly different. It was time to move on and try a new approach with people who could help me in the way I needed.

Where are you struggling and need to ask for help?

People often avoid asking for help out of fear of being seen as weak and unable to cope. In fact, asking for help is a sign of strength. It shows that you accept the boundaries of your capabilities and recognise that a team can be stronger when supporting each other.

How can you create a culture where people feel safe to ask for help?

When my clients work with horses, if someone is unable to move a horse, the rest of the team often feel uncomfortable watching. It is common for the team observing to want to offer support, but they often hold back for fear of not knowing whether an offer of help would be accepted, not knowing how to help and not wanting to diminish or insult the person they can see struggling. Nobody wants to watch others struggle. The person leading often doesn't consider asking for help because they would label it as a failure.

"Not knowing" is a concept that so many leaders struggle with. They desire certainty and answers, yet there is little certainty and no perfect answer in an economic environment requiring disruption, innovation and collaboration. People fear asking for help as much as they struggle to offer it, because offering and asking for help create further uncertainty in relationship. Uncertainty requires vulnerability, a willingness to work things through together, a leap of faith into the unknown in partnership. Most people find it easier to struggle on their own than to step into the vulnerability of relying on others for help.

Following a discussion on this, teams learn to offer support instead of diving in and taking over. They learn to be willing to have the offer rejected, as well as learn to ask for help from others more readily in return. By being open and transparent in the conversation around support and help, teams discover how to be in relationship in uncertainty. They work together better, speed up success and minimise failure and discomfort for everyone. Asking for help can be transformative for both individuals and teams.

Work-related stress

Leading through uncertainty requires a willingness to work as a team to explore answers together. Everyone wants to feel safe. In work situations where physical safety is paramount, e.g. manufacturing or construction industries, employees are used to talking about safety. It is a critical component of the job. In other industries that are office based, people rarely talk about safety in the workplace, and yet it is a key driver for how people operate. The rise of mental health issues and the shift to being able to talk about them is creating change in this area, but it's slow.

Whenever you operate out of your comfort zone, it feels unsettling. This can range from feeling slightly uncomfortable trying something new to severe overwhelm due to a high workload, a bullying manager or a new job where you don't feel capable of meeting the objectives.

Everyone's workload is ever-increasing. There is a limit to the capacity that the human brain can cope with. You are not a machine! Technology has limits and so does the human race. We are limited by our processing capabilities – both mental and physical. We are reaching a crisis point of human capacity, and something needs to shift to enable us to work more effectively.

How do you prioritise between what is urgent and what is important when everything appears to be both? How do you set realistic targets and objectives and recognise that people are human and are doing their very best? How do you balance that with the needs of shareholders who want better results and more money? These are fundamental questions that need to be asked.

We need to set people realistic targets that are within their capabilities. For almost two decades, the pressure people have been put under has been increasing, and it's time to take a look at what is actually achievable.

What targets are you driving towards that are unrealistic? What needs to happen?

We can redress the balance and find ways of working more efficiently, using technology to aid us with faster processing power. The current situation of faster processing power fuelling more human workload is not sustainable.

As more organisations downsize and the volume of workload increases, people are put under greater pressure to deliver more with fewer resources. Deadlines are increasingly unrealistic, and the incessant pressure escalates stress levels in the organisation. In parallel, technology is increasing the volume of information available, exacerbating the overwhelm. Many people are on conference calls all day, with no breaks in between. While listening (tentatively) to the call, they are processing emails, instant messages and social media, as well as writing documents and so on. This multi-tasking is not only highly ineffective, it is also damaging to people's health.

Many people are operating under severe pressure, with a sense of "If I can just get to the end of the week, it'll be ok". This is an adrenaline-fuelled, high-alert state, and people do not function effectively when placed under continual stress in this way. It also has huge implications on long-term physical and emotional health. People are trying to go faster and faster, caught up in the whirlwind of information, stopping only at the point of sheer exhaustion, overwhelm and, ultimately, burnout.

Overwhelm

In parallel to the increased workload, responsibilities outside of the workplace are growing too, such as childcare, parental care, the rise of dementia and an ageing population. All of these things affect employees. External stresses impact organisations. The two are inextricably linked because the people working in organisations are those same people who have external pressures. In the days of 9–5 work where people switched off and turned their attention to their personal life, it was easier to juggle the external pressures. Now, with the continual connection via technology, it is increasingly difficult to separate work and life.

As people feel continually under pressure and on auto-pilot to achieve everything they need to achieve in their lives and work, they lack the time to look after themselves in the process. It requires time to plan healthy meals, cook and do regular exercise. These are often aspects that fall to the bottom of the list of priorities, yet they have an impact on physical *and* emotional health. The delays in travelling to work, battling traffic, dealing with motorway closures or coping with a packed underground system in major cities exacerbate the frustration that people feel when they are under pressure.

More parents work full-time, and therefore the tension between work and life pressures is growing. Parents often use annual leave to cover childcare. As life expectancy rises, more people are also taking responsibility for parents and dealing with the added stress of dementia.

> *One in four people will have a mental health issue in the next 12 months, largely driven by unsustainable pressure and stress. The rapid pace of change is here to stay, and leadership has a critical role to play in how people are led and supported in this fast-changing and diverse world.*

In a 2017 HSE report, it was highlighted that "Work-related stress, depression or anxiety accounts for 40% of work-related ill health and 49% of working days lost in 2016/17. The reasons cited as causes of work-related stress are also consistent over time with workload, lack of managerial support and organisational change as the primary causative factors".[2] These statistics don't even include the physical health problems caused by stress.

Everyone responds to pressure in different ways. For many, the fear of getting things wrong is real. The consequences are substantial, too – missed promotions, blame, criticism and potential redundancy. These are genuine fears that cause people to put themselves under huge pressure, accepting the challenge they've been set whether they feel capable or not.

Organisations with a culture of fear and bullying have poor leadership and high levels of stress, overwhelm and burnout. Sadly, there are many organisations that do have such a culture, whether they like to admit it or not. There is a tendency to think that workplaces are far better today than in the Victorian era of poor factory conditions. While physical environments are vastly improved, the emotional stress and strain people are put under

---

[2] HSE, Work-related stress, depression or anxiety statistics in Great Britain 2017, HSE (2017). Available from: www.hse.gov.uk/statistics/causdis/stress/stress.pdf [accessed 18 March 2018].

repeatedly is an increasing and long-term societal problem which business must act upon.

Where are the stress points in your business?

Who needs your support?

Yorkshire Water, a utility company in the UK, has recognised the importance of leadership and the impact it has on mental health in the organisation. The occupational health team work closely with the business to ensure that mental health training is available to all line managers, as well as exploring how leadership behaviours impact levels of stress in the workplace. Substantial support is available for those feeling stressed, with the ultimate aim of reducing work-related stress and improving mental health.

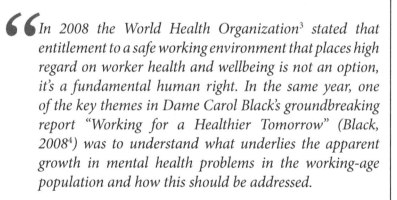

In 2008 the World Health Organization[3] stated that entitlement to a safe working environment that places high regard on worker health and wellbeing is not an option, it's a fundamental human right. In the same year, one of the key themes in Dame Carol Black's groundbreaking report "Working for a Healthier Tomorrow" (Black, 2008[4]) was to understand what underlies the apparent growth in mental health problems in the working-age population and how this should be addressed.

[3] World Health Organization, WHO Healthy Workplace Framework and Model (2008). Available from: www.who.int/occupational_health/ healthy_workplace_framework.pdf [accessed 18 March 2018].

[4] C. Black, Working for a healthier tomorrow, Department for Work and Pensions (2008). Available from: www.gov.uk/government/ uploads/system/uploads/attachment_data/file/209782/hwwb-working-for-a-healthier-tomorrow.pdf [accessed 20 January 2018].

The report stated that it was vital for employers to understand the importance of the role they have in preventing ill health and how workplace interventions can significantly contribute to the wider public health agenda, and in doing so not only reduce the burden on the NHS and the taxpayer but also support their own sustainability.

Ten years on, the Stevenson/Farmer Review of Mental Health and Employers (2017)[5] has taken employer responsibility for safeguarding the mental health of their employees to the next level. The report goes one step further from the rhetoric of the inspirational Black Report, which prompted organisations to act in a moral and ethical way to demonstrate corporate social responsibility. It takes the bold approach of recommending that the government set out clear expectations of employers through legislation.

Work intensification, a culture of long hours (the British worker has the longest working week in Europe), technology and the pace of change in the workplace leave employees with little capacity to cope with the mounting pressures in their lives outside of work. Employees come to work with a variety of life pressures already weighing on them heavily, such as caring responsibilities, grown-up children who can't afford to leave home, debt, relationship issues, to name but a few. It would be a triumph over reality for employers to expect them simply to leave their

---

[5] D. Stevenson and P. Farmer, Thriving at work: The Stevenson/Farmer Review of Mental Health and Employers, HMSO (2017). Available from: www.gov.uk/government/uploads/system/uploads/attachment_data/file/658145/thriving-at-work-stevenson-farmer-review.pdf [accessed 18 March 2018].

problems at the door, but in 21st-century Britain this expectation is no longer sustainable.

At Yorkshire Water we have taken some significant steps to protect the mental health of our employees. We have made it mandatory for all managers to undertake the two-day Mental Health First Aid course, and we have made it mandatory for every team to do a stress risk assessment, so that every employee has a voice. Employees who report being stressed at work or report sick because of stress are referred to occupational health on day one of doing so. We have formed a mental health support group so that employees can share their experiences and support each other, and we have a proactive approach to rehabilitating employees back to work. We also offer referral to an independent consultant psychiatrist and referral to a variety of talking therapies.

As a result, we have seen increased referrals to occupational health and our employee survey indicates that our employees feel supported and valued.

—Susan Gee, Occupational Health, Yorkshire Water

Workload, pressure, stress and overwhelm are different for everyone. It's unreasonable to expect everyone to cope with the same workload, just as some people are more capable of doing one job than another. Putting people under severe stress for prolonged periods leads to burnout. Once someone has experienced burnout in the workplace, it is very difficult to bring them back to the same job and expect them to perform. People are more likely to walk away than face it head on.

We need more dialogue around what is an acceptable level of pressure and a willingness to ease an unrealistic workload. Understanding individuals' capabilities related to stress and pressure is crucial to maximising productivity and minimising stress. It is not acceptable to continually put employees under substantial long-term pressure without accepting the responsibility for their mental health in the process.

Resilience

With the increasing pace and prevalent stress, there is a need to support yourself, as well as your team and organisation. It's important to recognise that you have limits. Those limits vary for everyone.

What's your limit and how do you know when you've reached it?

Overwhelm can tip you over the edge

Unrealistic targets and expectations are a major cause of stress and overwhelm. The increased uncertainty raises stress levels through the fear of the unknown and the fear of failure. Uncertainty is now a key part of everyday working life, and we need to equip leaders to manage their fear and reduce their stress. If you are conscious of when you are in a high period of stress, it is important to counteract this with time out and quieter periods of work. Raising awareness of the level of stress is essential to prevent it spiralling out of control.

Many organisations provide training in resilience and mindfulness, and this can be enormously helpful in retraining your thought processes to reduce stress and prevent overwhelm. However, some organisations use resilience as an excuse to put people under even more pressure, the implication being that the fault lies with the employee's response to pressure if they seem unable to cope. Wellbeing interventions should not be the antidote to excessive pressure, unrealistic workload and poor leadership. Wellbeing of a team is the responsibility of every leader in the organisation.

Where are you putting people under pressure, and how does that contribute to stress?

Consideration must be given to what is a reasonable and acceptable amount of pressure and this will vary on an individual basis. If we continue to demand more than people are able to deliver on a long-term basis, overwhelm, stress and burnout will continue their upward trend.

People can and do bounce back once they reach overwhelm, but it can take a long time for people to return to work when they have been absent with stress. The tendency to continually push through causes long-term damage on both a physical and a mental level. Learning where your limits are and keeping an open dialogue with your team is essential to understand the early warning signs of stress.

Stress is not just a mental health issue – the long-term health implications are significant, with many physical illnesses caused by stress. Wellbeing of the workforce is a responsibility of the organisation and is a leadership issue.

MASTERING UNCERTAINTY

- Ask for help. People want to provide support.

- Offer support to others and be willing to have it rejected without taking it as a personal affront.

- Create an environment of openness and transparency so your team feel comfortable asking for help.

- Be aware of your limits and the limits of others, and recognise that they may be very different.

- Take time out to recharge and encourage others to do the same to prevent being under continuous stress.

- Stop when you feel overwhelmed and find a new approach.

- Set realistic targets and challenge those that are not.

- Provide an environment of openness so people can monitor their stress and be honest about it.

Before you move on to the next chapter, spend 10 minutes reflecting on how stress and overwhelm influence you and your team.

 Download the *Leading Through Uncertainty* workbook from www.judejennison.com/uncertainty and record your reflections.

PROVOKING PERSONAL INSIGHT

Where are you struggling and need to ask for help?

How can you create a culture where people feel safe to ask for help?

What targets are you driving towards that are unrealistic? What needs to happen?

Where are the stress points in your business?

Who needs your support?

What's your limit and how do you know when you've reached it?

Where are you putting people under pressure, and how does that contribute to stress?

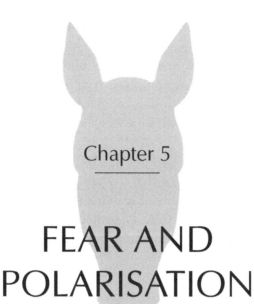

Chapter 5

FEAR AND POLARISATION

"Resistance is feedback that someone's
needs are not being met."

"I don't see the point of this, and I don't want to be here," Simon said as he walked through the gate and brushed past me in the office doorway. He was the last person to arrive. Everyone looked a little uncomfortable and shifted in their seats.

"That's OK," I replied without judgement and pointed him in the direction of the tea and coffee. Everyone breathed a sigh of relief as I let the moment pass.

We could not have been further apart in our views of working with horses. I have watched clients work with horses and gain major aha moments that transform everything in their life and work. I've seen how the horses help clients turn a loss-making business into a profit. Simon had not. He had no reference point. He was out of his comfort zone, on the verge of overwhelm. The truth is, he was scared, and his overconfident resistance was his way of staying safe. It was pointless trying to persuade him with words. Anything I said in that moment to try to convince him of the value of working with the horses would only increase the divide.

The horses win people round quickly, so I held Simon gently in his resistance, accepting that his perspective was true for him in that moment. When his time came to work with the horses, he opted to work with Kalle as people who are terrified often do. While many are intimidated by her self-assuredness and self-confidence, the ones who are overwhelmed often choose to work with her, as if they sense that she also has the capacity to be extremely gentle with anyone who is scared.

Simon took the lead rope from me and stroked Kalle on the neck. He took one step forward, invited her to walk with him, and off they went together. Kalle didn't challenge him any more than I had. She recognised that he needed to be put at ease, to be supported out of his comfort zone and held gently. He came back with a big smile on his face. Simon was achieving success as he perceived it by getting the horse to go with him. He was starting to move from his original position of fear and polarisation to meeting me and the horses in a place of curiosity and quiet, confident leadership.

Resistance

The cause of all resistance is fear, and it is prevalent in organisations and society. Uncertainty creates fear – fear of the unknown, fear of failure, fear of being vulnerable, fear for your safety. Fear makes you say and do things you would not normally say and do. It shows up as opposition, confrontation or unwillingness. It is your body and mind's way of keeping you safe and preventing failure.

Fear has a major role to play in your survival. With the ever-increasing uncertainty of life and work, fear is a prevalent emotion in our society today. Somehow, we need to find a way to recognise it and navigate it. The uncertainty of our time is here to stay, and we need to continually develop our skills to cope.

Uncertainty requires a new approach. When you loosen your attachment on a specific outcome or view of success, fear reduces and you find your flow of leadership.

When resistance shows up, either in you or in others, be curious about what is behind it. What are you afraid might happen? What are you wanting to avoid? Let go of blame and judgement and allow the resistance to be part of the process of people making sense of their fear or discomfort.

Simon's fear drove his behaviour. At his core, he is not a rude person, yet his behaviour may have appeared as such to some people because he was so far out of his comfort zone and almost at a place of overwhelm. He didn't see the point of what he was there to do and resisted it as much as he possibly could. In that moment, I had two choices: to meet him head on and try to persuade him, or to give him space to work it out for himself. I chose the latter.

In moments of resistance and polarisation, there is a tendency to resort to force to get people to come with you, instead of allowing them free will to work it out. Resistance needs space for understanding and reflection. This is born out of attachment to specific outcomes and breaks down relationships. Simon later admitted to being resistant at work in times of change or uncertainty. He was uneasy being out of his comfort zone, and his resistance was a natural response to keeping him safe in the status quo. Once he had time to work things out, he was an active and willing participant and team member.

When you lead a team, using rank and authority to make people come with you works to a point, but it's not leadership: it's coercion, force, command and control. Call it what you will, but it serves only to deepen the divide, erode trust and break down relationships. The end result is either that people feel coerced and give in, not through free will but through a need for harmony and resolution, or they fight and become forceful in return. This results in stalemate and deadlock.

Whenever we meet resistance, the tendency is to blame the other party, to judge them as stubborn or difficult rather than seeking to understand. Often clients will call the horse stubborn if the horse does not come willingly. I explain that they have not yet met the conditions that allow the horse to feel compelled to come with them willingly, and the horses won't come through force or rank. Resistance is feedback that someone's needs are not being met, but often we don't see this in the heat of the moment. Frustration during polarisation builds to a crescendo, escalating the coercion and corresponding resistance. The more you try to drag a horse, the more it digs its heels in. The same is true of people.

I often say to my clients, "My money is on the (600 kg) horse if you get into a tug of war!" Horses are physically stronger than us so they demonstrate how force doesn't work and invite people to find a different way of leading that is more relational, based on curiosity, collaboration and understanding.

When a horse refuses to come with you, the only option is to recalibrate and find another way. Clients discover greater flexibility and adaptability, as well as increased self-awareness, all of which are enormously useful in the workplace.

Resistance is futile... or is it?

With the pressure to deliver results in short timescales, stress behaviours are prevalent, especially in moments of uncertainty. People often resort to coercion to get the job done when they feel under pressure. Contrary to what you are trying to achieve by pushing for results, making specific demands leads to disengagement and further resistance and slows down results even more.

> *The resistance to change is a reflection of the desire for certainty and the status quo. There is a balance between not treating people as victims of their circumstances and recognising that not everyone can embrace uncertainty and change at the same pace.*

I explain in *Leadership Beyond Measure* why resistance shows up: "If you're getting resistance, people are effectively trying to say: 'It's too big a challenge for me, and I'm scared.'

Those people need help to navigate change and still feel safe" (Jennison, 2015[6]).

Ultimately resistance needs to be met with more space for curiosity and reflection. When you allow time for increased observation and understanding, relationships grow stronger and minimise the divide. That's challenging when you are under pressure to meet tight deadlines. Everyone will work at different paces and giving people space to work at their own pace is critical to minimise the resistance and reduce the polarisation.

What are you resisting and what impact is that having?

Where do you need to give people more space to work things out?

The desire for certainty

The resistance to change is often born out of the desire to hang on to what is known, understood and controllable, but control is fundamentally different from leadership. Certainty is more comfortable than uncertainty and therefore people naturally seek it as a way of staying safe. The desire for certainty is often expressed in the pursuit of wanting to be "in control" as if it were the panacea of creating success. People are comfortable with what they know because they have experience to handle it and think they cannot fail. In fact, certainty stifles creativity and innovation and prevents you from exploring alternative ways of doing things.

Where are you striving to be in control to avoid the discomfort of uncertainty?

Being in control does not allow for diverse opinions, dialogue and collaboration, and the desire for control further amplifies fear. Leaders who are comfortable with uncertainty are less likely

---

[6] J. Jennison, Leadership Beyond Measure, Createspace (2015).

to be afraid of the unknown. We can and must upskill leaders to have the self-confidence to lead through uncertainty and the willingness to step into the unknown.

Many organisations have a fear culture, born out of the desire for certainty. The incessant striving to achieve results under pressure has led to people being terrified of making mistakes for fear of the repercussions. Jobs are no longer for life, and there is less certainty about your position. Even highly skilled employees can find themselves caught up in a redundancy situation as companies consolidate and reorganise to reduce costs. The continuous fear of failure can be exhausting and drains your energy.

Where is fear impacting the behaviour of you or your team?

In periods of uncertainty, there is often a lack of information or knowledge, and there are multiple views about what is true. Facts become sketchy and people try to package bad news as good news. Many organisations presented the end of the final-salary pension as a way of helping people keep their jobs for longer. While there is an element of truth in this, it ultimately lacks honesty and integrity and implies that people are wrong for feeling angry or hard done by.

Fear and resistance can be exhausting. Change is often thrust upon us, and in those moments of uncertainty, the way forward may be unclear. When we trust that we can navigate whatever might be thrown our way, we can relinquish the hold that fear has on us and lead more powerfully in any given moment.

A management consultant from Newcastle, England, explained: "With the demise of manufacturing and shipbuilding in the north-east of England, I wasn't able to follow the same career path that my family had followed for decades. My future in work was uncertain, and that was terrifying and dispiriting. In hindsight, I realise it gave me the freedom to choose my own career elsewhere. At the time it didn't feel as though I was being freed up, it felt as though I was being pushed through adversity, and it was extremely uncomfortable."

Fear of the unknown and anxiety about the future are normal responses to the uncertainty people face through major change. Opportunities can be created out of adversity, but at the time people often feel anxious about the uncertainty of their future because the path to success and safety is unclear.

Adversity is an opportunity to create a new future, based on new insights and information. As we lead through uncertainty, organisations need to shift the culture from one of perfection and control to one of exploration and co-creation. If we do not let go of the need to control, we become polarised in our views with others, as everyone has a different point of view on how to move forward.

Polarisation

Polarisation occurs in situations where there is no obvious answer and where there are high levels of fear. The Leave and Remain campaigns for Brexit in the UK in June 2016 were both driven by fear and led to a period of high anxiety and polarisation that had ripples on a global scale. UK citizens were severely divided before, during and after the Brexit decision, with information being driven by emotional outbursts on both sides and a lack of understanding of the facts that were at the centre of the debate.

In moments of polarisation, facts often disappear and debates become emotional. Information becomes twisted and people use manipulation to try to get agreement.

The media often exacerbate polarised views through blame, criticism and judgement, which creates further tension and increases people's fear. Even established and well-respected programmes such as *Newsnight* on the BBC showcase polarisation and heated debate in which nobody is truly heard. In the absence of a balanced view and in a desire to make their point be accepted as the *only* truth, participants debate vociferously without listening to each other. True listening requires our view to be open to being changed by the perceptions of others by seeking new information.

Where are you polarised with someone and what are you not hearing?

Without dialogue, polarised views create further divide and deepen the fear. While this is obvious in world issues, it is also played out in organisations, where departments and teams go head to head, wanting their opinions to be understood and adhered to, without seeking to understand the challenges of the other. In such situations, there is no sense of a shared goal but a polarised sense of us and them. The desire for certainty causes rifts that are difficult to resolve without a new way of leading.

Black/white, yes/no and left/right answers are rarely possible or even desirable. When people go head to head, excessive amounts of time and energy are wasted and relationships break down further.

Embracing differences

Voicing diverse opinions often creates polarisation if it is done in an unskilled way. The attachment to being right causes people to force their own opinion on others, often through coercion or, even worse, through manipulative and subversive means. Diverse teams are more innovative and creative as different opinions are considered; however, the desire to be heard and understood makes it difficult to operate with differences of opinion. Differences in religion, race, gender, sexuality, age and much more can lead to polarisation if people are not skilled in engaging in dialogue.

We all have unconscious biases and we need to create space to allow those differences to be expressed and understood, without negating them as right or wrong based on our own bias. Curiosity is crucial in seeking to understand. A fast-paced, high-pressure working environment is not conducive to creating space to allow this to occur, which is why polarised views often remain.

When people take time to carefully consider important issues from a variety of angles, they can identify and adopt the best scenario. The continuous pressure that people feel under is not conducive to reflection and collaborative debate but is needed to reduce the polarisation and fear.

Aligned teams always get better results. Many organisations are complex, with a matrix-managed system that has conflicting goals and objectives. While the overall company vision may be clear, the execution of that vision on an individual and team basis is often less so. Multiple competing targets cause conflict on both an individual-to-individual basis and between organisational departments.

Tension around goals is often ignored and glossed over, and this can derail and delay achieving results. Attachment to specific outcomes prevents a willingness to consider alternative points of view. Alignment occurs through human connection, which can heal divides and relieve tension, but people tend to disconnect in times of disagreement. We need to give people the skills to work through differences and stay connected when the situation is uncomfortable.

Where is tension occurring for you and what outcome are you attached to?

What happens when you release your attachment and become more open and curious?

Case study – John*

John stood in the arena with Tiffin, who was running loose. John asked Tiffin to move away from him. Tiffin took off round the arena with explosive energy, bucking and rearing. John had no idea that his energy was so strong. He had freaked Tiffin out with his mere presence and driven him instantly to a place of fear. I asked John to drop his energy and help Tiffin calm down. John dropped his energy and Tiffin stopped.

For the next few minutes, Tiffin alternated between the extremes of being explosive and not moving, depending on John's energy. Finally, John stabilised his energy and found a place of flow without fear. Tiffin moved calmly around the arena, matching John step for step. They had found a place of connection and harmony.

Afterwards, John explained: "I thought people knew that I cared about them." His team said that they did, but that they also experienced his leadership as on or off and that they were often afraid to speak their truth. John was horrified. "Why didn't you tell me?"

"I was afraid you would not listen," came the reply.
* Name changed to protect confidentiality

When the pressure is on to deliver, human connection is one of the first things to suffer. Organisations spend huge amounts of time and money measuring the achievement of financial and numerical targets, and less time understanding the cost of disconnected individuals and teams and misaligned targets. The pursuit of targets influences where leaders put their attention and drives leadership behaviour to focus on results rather than on relationships and connection. High-performing teams recognise the importance of embracing differences and not taking things personally. They allow constructive debate and know that connection and relationships are crucial to their success.

Clarity is essential when setting targets to understand the expectations of people with differing needs. We often use the same words to mean different things, and this is magnified further when working across cultures in different languages.

Embracing differences requires acceptance of self and others, even when opinions are different. Check that you are receptive to connection with others with differing views, opinions and beliefs. It is possible to connect through differences of opinion when respect and trust are at the heart of the connection and when people create an environment of openness, flexibility and curiosity.

The wisdom of fear

We must not stay stuck in the loop of fear and polarisation. We no longer live in tribal villages, where everyone knows their neighbour and has shared experience, values and belief systems. We work in a global economy where things are shifting, technology is influencing the way we work, and we work with people with different values and belief systems. This diversity enables us to learn from each other by exploring new ideas and ways of working. We can shape the future of work as well as society when we work collaboratively, but that's easier said than done.

> *Fear has its place. It can be useful as a source of information to identify the things you need to take care of, to identify potential risks and to find ways to mitigate them.*

We rarely consider the wisdom of fear. Fear is an innate emotional response to a situation that puts our safety at risk.

Instead of squashing the emotion, fear can inform us and cause us to pay attention to something that we might not otherwise expect. When we pay attention to fear as a source of information, we can manage its impact. We need space to process how we feel about things. Emotional intelligence is crucial to reducing polarisation in the workplace, and it starts by understanding your own fear and making sense of it in some way.

What is the inherent need you have that fear is pointing to?

When your team are resistant and fearful, there is a tendency to drag them along. The focus on the end goal prevents people having time and space to reflect and process. When people understand what change means for them, they can make sense of it and choose a different response that meets their needs.

> *Fear and polarisation are part of the human experience and an emotional response to protect ourselves and meet our needs. They inform us that there are fundamental differences of opinion.*

When we shift from a culture of fear and polarisation to one of hope, opportunity and exploration, we allow all the voices to be heard and expressed through dialogue. We can't shift from it fully, however. Fear and polarisation are a flag to remind you to pay attention to what needs to happen next in service of the bigger picture. That includes your needs as well as the needs of others. Fear is not going to go away. It is a fundamental part of leading though uncertainty, of stretching out of the comfort zone and pushing the boundaries of what is possible. We can, however, manage the incessant pressure more effectively, and this requires a new set of leadership skills and behaviours that I'll explore in more detail in Part 3 of this book.

MASTERING UNCERTAINTY

- Let go of attachment to specific outcomes.

- Be curious about resistance and seek to understand it without blame or judgement.

- Provide time and space for reflection when there is resistance.

- Swap control for leadership.

- Trust in the emerging future, especially if you do not have all the facts and information available.

- Worry only about the things you can change.

- Encourage dialogue where there are polarised views.

- Embrace differences of opinion by accepting and respecting self and others.

Before you move on to the next chapter, spend 10 minutes reflecting on where fear and polarisation show up in your organisation and how you can navigate it more effectively.

 Download the *Leading Through Uncertainty* workbook from www.judejennison.com/uncertainty and record your reflections.

PROVOKING PERSONAL INSIGHT

What are you resisting and what impact is that having?

Where do you need to give people more space to work things out?

Where are you striving to be in control to avoid the discomfort of uncertainty?

Where is fear impacting the behaviour of you or your team?

Where are you polarised with someone and what are you not hearing?

Where is tension occurring for you and what outcome are you attached to?

What happens when you release your attachment and become more open and curious?

What is the inherent need that you have that fear is pointing to?

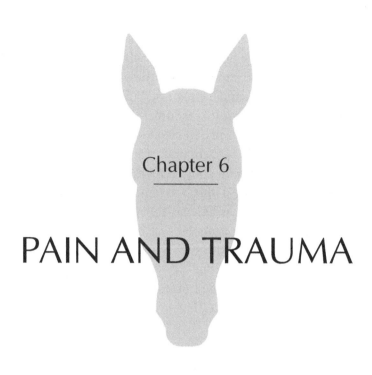

Chapter 6

PAIN AND TRAUMA

*"Pain and trauma are part of the human condition,
and our past experiences influence our leadership
on a day-to-day basis."*

Tiffin reared up, his eyes wild in fear and his legs flailing high above my head. My heart rate shot up, and I jumped back to avoid being kicked. The rope snapped as Tiffin pulled away from the fence, and he was free. He charged off down the yard towards the gate into the field, his head high, snorting in terror. I followed him cautiously, terrified of being trampled or kicked.

Tiffin stood at the gate and I took hold of the lead rope. His heart was racing, and mine mirrored his, each of us fearing for our safety. I'm no match for a 600 kg horse who has lost all sense of reason, especially when my heart is pounding and I'm in overwhelm too. He danced on his toes, snorting and blowing hard. I couldn't remove his head collar when he was in this state, so I unclipped the lead rope, opened the gate and let him go. He needed to move his feet and be free, and I needed to bring my heart rate down so I could be more resourceful. Within a few minutes, Tiffin was calm again as the perceived danger and fear subsided. I calmed down, too, but I remained cautious in handling him, knowing that the explosion could return another day.

This was the first time Tiffin had behaved in this way. He had been with me for six months, and throughout that time he had been sweet, gentle and willing. He was doing amazing work with clients and was engaged with me in between. I'd always thought he was easy to handle until that day when I realised he was more complex. I had tied up all the horses to groom them for a photo shoot. It's a rare occurrence that my horses are tied up on the yard, and even more rare that they are all tied up in a line. I think it reminded him of his racing days, and he panicked.

In the brief moment that Tiffin reared up, both his trauma of being beaten on a race yard and my trauma of being unsafe with a rearing horse were invoked. We were wary of each other for the next few months, wanting to trust each other, knowing that deep down we were both kind and meant well, but both terrified for our safety. Tiffin's size, strength and unpredictability had the potential to seriously injure me if he exploded again. I was sure he wouldn't hurt me on purpose, but he could do so easily in a moment of panic when he was not thinking clearly. Tiffin had no intention of rearing again any more than I would slap him, but it took a few months of learning to trust that we could be safe together before we could relax again.

Triggering learned behaviours

At every moment, there will be people in your organisation who are suffering with mental health issues, loss or grief, people who have physical injuries, disabilities, or medical issues such as heart failure or cancer. These things affect our leadership. We can't leave all of that behind. If you are in the midst of loss or have severe back pain, or you have a parent with dementia or a child with cancer, you can't expect to operate at your peak performance level. Human beings experience emotions. That means we are affected by physical and emotional trauma. It's unreasonable to expect anybody who is going through those things to disappear out of the workplace or self-manage it so that it doesn't have an impact.

You may think that pain and trauma have more to do with therapy than leadership. I include these in this book because they have a major impact in the workplace and are largely unspoken. People believe it is wrong to express their emotions in the workplace so they learn to suppress them instead of using them skilfully. Yet emotions, pain and trauma fundamentally change the way we behave and therefore lead, and this change is largely unconscious for most people. Everyone is influenced by pain and trauma at some point in their lives. While you may not yet have experienced pain or trauma, it is important as a leader to recognise where it might be influencing others.

Uncertainty puts us under stress. How comfortable you are with uncertainty will determine how much stress you feel. Past pain and trauma are closer to the surface in these moments, and it is much easier to be triggered by seemingly small events when you are already agitated.

Negative experiences, both physical and emotional, linger in our memory over a long period of time, often without us being aware of them. They are part of the human condition, and everyone will experience them at some point in their lives. Learned behaviours and responses to pain and trauma affect all of us and shape how we walk in the world. To ignore this in business belies the core of our humanity.

We can be triggered by events that remind us (often subconsciously) of past pain and trauma because we invoke a desire to be safe. If we are unconscious of being triggered, we may experience emotional outbursts that appear to be out of proportion to the current event but are triggered by something deeper, as with Tiffin taking me by surprise. When on the receiving end of these outbursts, we often judge the person as "out of control" or "not emotionally intelligent" when in fact they are operating at the limit of their stress and need our support.

Where do **you** *get triggered?*

> *Uncertainty is deeply uncomfortable for people, yet it is the new normal. The continuous pressure of being out of your comfort zone requires new skills and greater resilience than ever before.*

Leaders need to increase flexibility and adapt to changing situations and environments without panicking. When events happen unexpectedly, they can be traumatic, e.g. for someone who has been rejected in the past, a forthcoming redundancy programme can trigger emotions around rejection. The fear of being made redundant may be greater for that person because they are scarred by the previous rejection experience, even if they are completely unaware of it.

When we make decisions, we make them based on our own set of experiences, often without taking into account the fact that others will have a different set of experiences.

> *If you've never experienced rejection or had a traumatic experience of any kind, you may not realise the impact that such an event can have and how it can emotionally trigger people's past pain and trauma.*

This is a leadership issue because leaders make decisions every day that affect others, without fully understanding the consequences. If we repeatedly put either ourselves or others under continuous stress without being aware of the consequences, we exacerbate mental health issues and risk burnout. The high pressure of most business environments often shifts the focus to achieving results, at the expense of the people. This has a major impact on the mental health of employees and it is not sustainable.

How do you balance meeting your targets and objectives while having compassion for the needs of your team?

When we raise our self-awareness around our default patterns of behaviour, we can choose more consciously the actions we take in future and stop being limited by our old (often unconscious) stories.

However you deal with past experiences, they affect your behaviour. When you are aware of your patterns of behaviour, you can make conscious decisions about how you show up and the actions you take. This is a lifelong process of learning.

Your experiences shape your world

The jobs you've done and the experiences you've had, both in your personal and your work life, shape how you show up as a leader and influence how you lead. If you've had a bad experience, a job role that has not worked out, been made redundant, or been told you are not performing as expected, there is learning in that, but there is also some baggage around what works, what doesn't and why.

Your experiences shape your leadership, and leadership shapes business. If you have been a high performer all your life and had great roles and excelled in every single one, that shapes your approach to the next role – you may be full of confidence because your leadership has been tried and tested and proved effective.

What past experiences shape your behaviour and impact your leadership?

Who in your team might be struggling with past experiences, and how can you support them?

By contrast, imagine you've performed a high-profile role that has not turned out well, for whatever reason. How does that shape or influence your next role? Does it dent your confidence or can you bounce back and recognise that the conditions for success were not in place?

With the pressure of work, decisions are often taken to remove people from roles instead of taking time to support them to learn new skills and do things differently. This has a huge impact on the confidence of highly skilled people as they find themselves pulled off projects at short notice, often with little discussion around how they could do things differently. If you do need to pull someone from a team, consider the long-term impact on the individual. Make it as painless as possible for them.

Every action you take as a leader can have a positive or negative impact on individuals. Consider how you can make this a more positive experience to boost their confidence instead of crushing it.

If you are on the receiving end of such a decision, you can choose how you respond and the perspective you take. You can accept all the blame for a poorly executed decision and let a moment of failure derail your whole approach, or you can see failure as a moment in time where something didn't work out as planned. This is what it means to be resilient – to bounce back from challenges, learn from the experience and move on.

While your experiences shape your approach, the same is true for every single person in the organisation. On one level, people bring with them all their work experience, success and confidence from previous roles. They also bring the pain of the challenges that they faced and didn't overcome, things they didn't do effectively, as well as mistakes they made and the impact that had on their career. How we respond to those mistakes and failures is crucial for our leadership.

How do you support others to recover from failure and prevent it from derailing their future?

Are you encouraging a culture of failure without blame or judgement, or do you write people off quickly?

There is huge learning to be had from these moments of pain and the challenges we experience *if* we choose to embrace that learning and explore how we can do things differently. Self-awareness is crucial to our leadership so that we can use our skills more readily and more consciously. By our very nature, we also sabotage our leadership and career, causing us to be stuck without realising it. All of our default habits and behaviours come with us, the ones that help us succeed as well as the pain and trauma that limit our leadership.

Case study – Colin*

Colin had blocked his past trauma and had no patience for anyone in his team. He had learned to suppress his emotional pain and expected others to do the same. As a result, he had no empathy for those who were struggling with high workload and on the verge of burnout. He had no idea that many of his team felt bullied.

When Colin worked with a horse called Kalle, he asked her to move. There was no empathy for her or space for her to have an opinion, so she refused and stood still. Colin became increasingly frustrated, but he tried to hide it. The more he tried to contain his anger, the more unwilling Kalle was to go with him. She refused to cooperate with either the anger or the suppression of it.

Colin realised, as many clients do, that his experiences were affecting his leadership. He didn't need to divulge the past trauma because the details were not relevant. Instead, we explored how it had resulted in his lack of empathy, which prevented him from building good relationships with his team. It was deeply insightful for Colin to realise the pressure he was putting on his team by refusing to give space for emotions and not acknowledging when people were struggling.

Colin had no intention of bullying his team, but his lack of empathy prevented him from supporting them under pressure. Since the workshop, Colin's relationships with the team have improved. They talk openly about the pressure they are under and work together to help alleviate it. Fear, blame, judgement and stress have all reduced within the team.

* Name changed to protect confidentiality

Empathy without derailing

We are not machines. We have human experiences, with emotional highs and lows. We tend to forget this when we continuously strive for end goals in business.

Tiffin's experience of poor treatment on a former racing yard has left its mark. He takes longer to build trust with people, especially men with strong, dominant energy. His workload is therefore lower than that of the other horses in the herd because he gets stressed more quickly. I pay closer attention to him to ensure he does not get overwhelmed and panic. By understanding him in this way and recognising his limits, he is able to continue working.

Although Tiffin's workload may be lower, his impact certainly is not. He will highlight emotional and physical pain in clients, a role he plays willingly, resulting in profound insights for them that the other horses could not provide. While Tiffin cannot do the workload of Kalle, he brings something that she cannot. Therein lies his value.

> *We cannot always measure the input and output of team members with tangible numerical metrics; we must also explore the value that people bring to the team that is unique to them and that nobody else could bring.*

When someone behaves out of character, there is usually a good reason and it may not be obvious. People are not always consistent in their behaviour because their experiences influence how they show up in different situations. When you pay greater attention to how people behave and their emotional responses, there is an opportunity to flex your style to get the best out of everyone in any given moment.

Tiffin shows no sign of trauma when he is relaxed and supported

It's important to have empathy for everyone in the organisation during times of major change and uncertainty, to recognise that people are affected in different ways and to help them navigate uncertainty. This is different for everyone. In my book *Leadership Beyond Measure*, I explain how the comfort zone affects different people in different ways. "If you find yourself stretching more and more in your work and you feel overstretched constantly, you need to take time out to relax and recharge. When people go off sick with work-related stress, it's because they have felt as though they are constantly in the danger zone and have not felt able to take time out".[7]

Organisational trauma

Pain and trauma are not limited to individuals. Repeated change and transformation cause organisational trauma. As we undergo rapid change, organisations respond through restructuring programmes, organisational change and redefining of people's roles. This increases uncertainty and has an emotional impact on the people in the organisation.

When a large proportion of a workforce is made redundant, it's not just those who leave who feel uncertain. Change has an impact on those left behind as they reorganise and adapt to meet the changing needs of the new organisation. There is a period of uncertainty as job roles change, and people potentially expand their responsibilities as they pick up the additional workload. The organisation and culture change as well. There is a grieving process (however minor) for those left behind as they say goodbye to colleagues they respected and enjoyed working with.

Everyone's job shifts, sometimes in small ways, sometimes substantially. Redundancy programmes don't just have an impact on the people who are made redundant; employees who remain

---

[7] J. Jennison, Leadership Beyond Measure, Createspace (2015).

are affected and the organisation undergoes trauma. Typically, this trauma is unspoken, unacknowledged and ignored.

Employees are often encouraged to think positively and look forward, meeting the new challenges with enthusiasm and positivity. We are expected to be happy at all times in order to engage and inspire others. This steps over the need to feel emotions and move on from them. In pretending the redundancy does not affect the remaining employees, the old unfinished situation is necessarily suppressed. People may feel anger (at how colleagues have been treated or how the process has been executed), fear (that they may have narrowly escaped losing their job and might lose it in future) or many other emotions.

The suppression of these emotions generates unrest within the organisation and creates a ripple effect. Suppressed emotions cause a lack of authenticity, which leads to mistrust in the organisation. Those who express their anger or fear are challenged and criticised for being emotional at work. We are expected to move on quickly. By stepping over our emotional experience, organisational trauma does not disappear, however. Instead, it becomes the unnamed influence that continues to have an impact, even though it is unacknowledged.

We need a level of honesty and transparency around organisational change. Emotions need space to be expressed, understood and recognised. This does not mean getting caught up in emotional outbursts and creating a downward spiral of righteous indignation. Instead it requires a recognition that everyone is having their own emotional experience and an acknowledgement that moving on can take more time. The trauma does not end on the day people leave the organisation, it continues to have an impact for weeks and months.

What trauma is affecting your organisation that is largely being glossed over?

It's not just traumatic events such as redundancy that create organisational trauma. Mergers and acquisitions, and any other forms of major change, also create trauma. Uncertainty in these moments is challenging and generates a whole range of emotions. How the organisation responds, and how people are supported through change, affects the company culture and the ability to move forward.

Some organisations operate on the front line and may be repeatedly operating under stress, for example the police, armed forces, ambulance services, or trading desks, where people run on adrenaline. Leaders in those organisations need to provide greater support to reduce stress and overwhelm and encourage people to be honest about their emotions. One great example of such a leader is Elizabeth Cronin, the Director of the New York State Office of Victim Services. She recognises the importance of empathy for her team and she finds ways to ease the pressure they are under.

> " *We are at the sharp end of uncertainty. I have to be mindful that my staff can be traumatised at any time. My team work with very difficult issues. We never know what is going to happen from one day to the next. We work with people who could be upset or traumatised. Each case is different.*
>
> *The New York State Office of Victim Services provides financial compensation to innocent victims of crime. We also fund victim assistance providers throughout the state of New York, and we advocate on behalf of crime victims throughout the state. It's a necessary component of a criminal justice response. Every claim is a person with a history, a family and a circumstance that has to be considered. My executive team and I help the team understand the mission and keep going back to it. Work is never just about processing something. It's essential to understand why you are doing it.*
>
> *This agency has had to respond to some terrible mass events like 9/11. In 2009 there was a mass shooting where*

many people were killed, severely injured and traumatised. We have to respond to those things as well as doing our regular day-to-day work. The caregivers need care as well as those who receive our services. We recognise that staff are dealing with very difficult things and need training and support on an ongoing basis. We cannot ignore the importance of this.

In addition, people are dealing with their own life experiences and trauma situations. We have to be open-minded and pay attention to staff. We do a lot of cross-training with other agencies so that they can seek support from other areas. We try to have a lot of fun, too, as an antidote to the serious issues we deal with. I recognise that people are doing very difficult work and need to let off steam. Our work is deadly serious, but we are all human beings and need to balance the severity and seriousness with light-heartedness as well.

People need to know that they are supported and understood and I work hard to do that with my team. I'm a fast thinker, so I pay attention to slow down, wait until someone has finished, allow a moment of silence to process ideas until they can articulate it. I need to know what's really happening on the ground and I can only do that by truly listening to people. When you listen to people, they feel valued and are more likely to come forward and tell you things you want to hear, but also the things you might not want to hear. It creates an environment of openness that is really needed when you are leading through uncertainty.

Leading through uncertainty presents challenges for all of us and I am mindful of the need to ensure everyone in my team is adequately supported. Only then can we achieve our mission together.

—Elizabeth Cronin, Director, New York State Office of Victim Services

MASTERING UNCERTAINTY

- Notice how different people respond to change and who needs your support.

- Be mindful of what is triggering you and others.

- Be curious with other people's emotional outbursts and explore the unmet needs.

- Be aware of your default patterns of behaviour.

- Consider the impact of your decisions on others.

- Empathise with and support those who may be suffering.

- Provide some stability during times of major change.

- Encourage open dialogue around organisational change to prevent trauma building up.

Before you move on to the next chapter, spend 10 minutes reflecting on how past experiences, pain and trauma influence you and your team.

 Download the *Leading Through Uncertainty* workbook from www.judejennison.com/uncertainty and record your reflections.

PROVOKING PERSONAL INSIGHT

Where do you get triggered?

How do you balance meeting your targets and objectives while having compassion for the needs of your team?

What past experiences shape your behaviour and impact your leadership?

Who in your team might be struggling with past experiences and how can you support them?

How do you support others to recover from failure and prevent it from derailing their future?

Are you encouraging a culture of failure without blame or judgement, or do you write people off quickly?

What trauma is affecting your organisation that is largely being glossed over?

Part 3
HUMAN CONNECTION

Chapter 7

CREATING THE FRAMEWORK

*"A framework provides familiarity and certainty
for people to cling to and offers some comfort in the
midst of uncertainty."*

"How do I lead (the horse)?"
   "Does it matter which side I lead from?"
   "Can I talk to the horse?"
   "Do I need to go clockwise or anti-clockwise round the arena?"
   "How do I hold the lead rope?"
   "Am I allowed to…?"
I often face a barrage of questions from clients when they arrive at the stables for a Leadership with Horses session. They are faced with the uncertainty of an unknown environment, with a new team, with a species they don't know or understand.

I set clear guidelines around physical safety so that people can manage their own safety, and I explain that it's their personal responsibility to determine their boundaries of emotional safety. That often comes as a surprise. I provide clear instructions on not standing behind a horse in case it kicks and not allowing a horse to chew clothing, but how people lead, how close they stand or what they tolerate is their responsibility because everyone will have different boundaries.

The need for certainty and clarity in moments of uncertainty is great. At one end of the scale, some people respond by asking lots of questions, terrified of making assumptions and getting it wrong. They need to know exactly how to do something to avoid failure. This can lead to paralysis and slow down the process of getting going. The fear of stepping out of the comfort zone prevents them from doing anything that they don't know how to do. If they are not sure how to do something, they hold back, unwilling to risk failure or their safety. There is a desire for someone else to articulate the boundaries and provide detailed guidelines to create a level of certainty and safety.

At the opposite end of the scale, other people dive in, with no knowledge or understanding, no framework and no clear idea of the expectations. They may make assumptions that are invalid or impose boundaries that prevent them from succeeding. They may not pay attention to what is happening around them, causing them to go off track, leading to prevarication and chaos. Sometimes, they have no boundaries, requiring me to repeatedly point out physical safety issues.

At one end of the spectrum is paralysis through fear, at the other is chaos and a lack of safety. Somewhere in between lies the framework for your leadership.

The balance of certainty and uncertainty

A balance is needed between certainty and uncertainty. It can feel as though there is no foundation if everything appears to be in chaos. There are always people, things and situations that are certain, and it is important to identify those things in moments of chaos and confusion. They provide a support structure. Creativity occurs at its best within a framework. In the absence of a framework, chaos ensues.

While researching for this book, I interviewed a number of CEOs from different sectors and businesses. A common theme among all of them was the recognition that things have always been uncertain and that we need the skills to navigate that uncertainty, but organisations are not clear what those skills are. Saying we need more leadership in business is common but is too vague, especially since there is no definitive view of what leadership is.

The pace of change makes us more aware of uncertainty. It is not a new phenomenon, but it is more prevalent than ever before.

Most of the CEOs I interviewed felt very comfortable navigating uncertainty, and some of them recognised that this was not the case for their employees. I asked them whether the absence of a boss influenced how comfortable they felt with uncertainty. Their response was that they were accountable to the stock market and shareholders and as such felt the pressure as much as anyone.

It became clear that there is something about the nature of a CEO that means they embrace change more readily than people at other levels of the organisation. Perhaps it has to do with them leading from the front and feeling more certain of the direction they are heading? They rarely experience a feeling of "being done to" that those at other levels of an organisation may experience.

Their greater certainty allows them to flex more easily, with more understanding and influence on what the framework is.

How can you create more certainty for you and your team as a framework for flexibility?

Where can you provide more clarity, direction and purpose?

When everything seems uncertain, many of the CEOs I interviewed looked for the things that were certain as a coping strategy to help them navigate the discomfort. In this way, they rarely felt that everything was in total turmoil; instead they relied on what was known and understood and used that as a foundation for moving forward into the unknown. They gained comfort from knowing that there were some things they could influence. They would focus on those things, trusting that they could handle the uncertain things when the time came.

We clearly need to balance certainty and uncertainty and find a way to embrace uncertainty without fuelling the discomfort.

Creating a framework

Balance and a framework enable teams to operate together effectively in times of uncertainty. Having clear boundaries and guidelines enables them to be agile and flexible, while providing safety and security for everyone. Uncertainty requires a new set of skills and a framework within which to flex and operate. In the absence of a defined vision, guidelines, boundaries and roles, teams encounter disconnection, disengagement, disagreements and confusion. Differences of opinion may lead to chaos, prevarication and lengthy meetings that go round and round with no clear outcome and no shared responsibility for success.

A framework during uncertainty helps leaders and teams lead with more ease and flow. It requires a presence and a willingness from each person to act in service of the whole, as well as an ability to self-manage in moments of discomfort. The desire for self-protection is in direct response to the vulnerability and discomfort of uncertainty. A loose framework that can be evolved by the group enables leadership to flow more easily and reduces the insecurity of not knowing.

The framework provides a level of clarity in the uncertainty, something that a team can hold on to, knowing the shared boundaries within which they can operate. This provides security and stability for people to cling to, reduces the vulnerability of being out of the comfort zone, and supports dialogue and conversation. There are many different ways of providing a framework – through values, guidelines for how the team work and clear expectations and objectives. The more clarity that you can provide in times of uncertainty, the more people can relax within what is unknown, as they have something to hang on to.

The primary leadership model I work with is called Three Positions of Leadership and it provides a framework for how a team can work. It is based on how a herd of horses operates naturally in the wild and maps onto what is needed for a high-performing human team. It consists of three primary roles:

1. **Leading from the front:** provides the clarity, direction and purpose (the "what", "where" and "why"), as well as setting the pace. A clear strategy and defined objectives make it easier to flex in the process (the "how").

2. **Leading from the middle:** this is the "how" and requires flexibility and communication. This is about execution and the middle is where the majority of the team work together, providing support for each other as and when they need it. It requires attention to the whole, as well as focus on where you are going.

3. **Leading from behind:** creates the momentum and helps everyone stay on track. The leader at the back can also see which parts of the team or organisation need more focus to stay on track and can provide support and guidance where needed.

All three positions are needed in a cohesive team. More details on this leadership model can be downloaded from my website in the form of a white paper. It is also explained more extensively in my book *Leadership Beyond Measure*.

 Download the Three Positions of Leadership model from www.judejennison.com/uncertainty

In an interview with Sondra Scott, president of Verisk Maplecroft, in 2017, she explained how she leads from the front: "I have one 'rallying cry' for my team that is the highest priority that my team focus on. It helps us have a framework that keeps people grounded. The framework provides the certainty within which we can flex. It's really hard to be flexible if you don't know what the boundaries are within which you are flexing. You need to be able to pivot quickly, so if you already understand the implications, you can act more quickly and be more flexible and agile."

Sondra's team understand the importance of working together towards a common goal or objective and that helps them navigate the uncertainty of the "how". Sondra went on to explain how her team lead from the middle: "People associate uncertainty with fear and see it as a bad thing. You can get paralysed if you don't conquer the fear. The best way to conquer that fear is to dissect it, understand it and identify the worst-case scenario. Then you can start to take action to protect yourself and reduce the risks. It becomes easier to lead once you have the scenarios mapped out because you know the worst-case scenario is avoidable."

A team provide unity and clarity for Kalle

However you build a framework, it sets the guidelines for how we work and what we do. Another key component of any framework is your personal values, which can guide you on how to operate. For example, when applying for a new role, you can decide whether the company is a good fit for you. Notice what language is used in the job description, as well as the interview and every interaction you have. If you have a value around collaboration and much of the conversation is around personal gain, there may be a mismatch. Your values set the tone for the team or organisation you lead as well as your own decisions and should be demonstrable in everyday actions.

Organisations often define company values that provide a framework for how people work. One of the challenges with this is that the reality does not always match the words that have been written. If you define values as a team or organisation, it is important to live and breathe them, otherwise trust is broken and the words are meaningless. For example, if the organisation has a value around innovation, there needs to be space for people to make mistakes and learn through trial and error.

Self-awareness

Uncertainty offers imperfect choices. There is no right or wrong way because uncertainty is by its very nature untried and untested. It provides an opportunity to try something new, pay attention to the results, recalibrate and modify where needed, in both the doing and the being. This level of flexibility can often feel at odds with meeting tangible goals and targets.

Senior leaders often tell me that they want their teams to think for themselves and be more self-sufficient, but they don't give them the space to do so. Empowerment requires space and time. It involves delegating effectively and trusting that people will find their own way, even when things don't go according to plan. Employees are rarely provided enough clarity and direction and even more rarely given the space to resolve issues in their own way. We need to shift from a culture of interfering when things go wrong to allowing space for people to work things out. When you provide a framework of clear boundaries, guidelines and values, there is an opportunity for people to work things out.

How do you embrace uncertainty in a way that does not add energy to the struggle but instead creates a framework for safety within which people can flex?

If we accept that uncertainty generates strong emotions, how do you equip leaders to be skilled in handling those emotions?

This is the challenge we face when leading through uncertainty. While uncertainty may generate strong reactions in those around you, it also impacts and influences *your* leadership. You are not immune from stress and fear, any more than anyone else is.

How do we encourage people to be human again in moments of uncertainty? When you encourage natural leadership and authentic behaviour to be present in every moment, you create a transparency that enables people to relax into their leadership, without the anxiety of needing to be the "perfect" leader.

How do you allow yourself to have emotions in relationships with others, knowing that your emotions influence your leadership?

People who lack self-awareness are often oblivious to the struggle of others around them. What can we learn from these people? They have a tendency to float through life, not necessarily being easy to work with, but they lack the anxiety that comes with self-awareness.

Self-awareness can create further anxiety as people try to behave as they believe they "should" behave. In the desire to be self-aware, we can increase the struggle of uncertainty as we aim to be the "perfect" leader. Self-awareness needs to be balanced with self-control and requires a letting go of blame, judgement and criticism, especially of yourself. The tendency towards self-flagellation has no place in leadership!

True self-awareness involves noticing the patterns of behaviour that we exhibit, the impact they have and then the choice to do something different if it is not what we want. The choices you make become the framework for operating in uncertainty. Your values and beliefs when articulated provide a structure for people to rely on.

Learning and growth start with self-awareness. Behavioural change can occur only when we deepen the awareness of how we behave and make choices about how we want to behave and the impact we want to have on others. When teams have the confidence and trust to give feedback without judgement, they help each other build self-awareness and develop new skills.

Case study – Financial Services company

A team came to work with the horses and found the learning enlightening. When they returned to the office, they used the shared experience as a framework for giving each other feedback without judgement or criticism.

Whenever someone said or did something that the rest of the team did not like, they would jokingly say, "I think if you were trying to move a horse right now, they would not come with you."

Everyone laughs, remembers the experience and the person concerned remembers how to flex their approach. It has become an office joke that relaxes everyone and relieves tension while giving feedback to try a different approach. It removes any judgement and allows the individual to decide how to change their style.

Self-control

In a fast-paced environment, it is easy to get caught up in the information and speed. Self-awareness and self-control enable leaders to pay attention to what is needed in service of the whole rather than driving one's own agenda.

When working with the horses, the desire to connect with the animals can often cause people to walk purposefully towards them. The horses can feel threatened by the intensity of this and often move away. By being aware of their impact, a team can slow down their pace and provide space for the horses to move towards them.

This demonstrates how we can create an environment where people want to belong and how we can attract the results we want, rather than constantly pushing and striving for them. Having a sense of purpose and attracting others towards that purpose generates results more organically and minimises stress on teams.

Self-control does not mean you have to suppress all of your immediate thoughts and feelings. It involves paying attention to your needs and the needs of others, and acting in service of the whole, i.e. speaking honestly about your own needs while respecting the needs of others.

Clear boundaries

Connection is not the same as relationship and friendship. It is important to be clear what you are wanting to create and why. People often avoid connection in the workplace because they fear becoming embroiled in a friendship that does not feel appropriate. In trying to set clear boundaries, people often create barriers and cause disconnection.

Connections can be created across a room full of people and may be as simple as a glance. It indicates a sense of deep knowing and seeing another person as they are, and it allows them to see you in that moment, too. Connection can be created at a deep level on a momentary basis and does not necessarily result in a long-term relationship or friendship. Once people realise that, they are less afraid of the intimacy of connection and are able to set boundaries rather than barriers.

Everyone will hold their boundaries differently. When leaders are clear and consistent with their boundaries, they create deeper levels of connection based on trust and respect, with the knowledge that they can communicate with clarity around their needs. Clear boundaries enable leaders to influence others without curbing or coercion. They articulate their needs, knowing that the connection goes beyond any challenges they are facing and allows them to reach alignment.

Often people relax their boundaries out of a desire to be flexible. Boundaries provide clarity around what is ok and what is not. If you flex your boundaries too much, others may take advantage of you and your needs may not be met. Alternatively, if you hold them too strongly, you may be seen as inflexible and difficult to collaborate with, and equally with this approach your needs will not be met either. Boundaries change as the organisation and world around you change, or as you gain new insights and information. Leaders who articulate their boundaries provide clarity and a structure for others to operate within. This creates a certainty within the uncertainty.

Boundaries provide the framework of what is acceptable behaviour and interaction, and they are essential in times of uncertainty. Boundaries are defined based on your values, beliefs and experience, and they may differ substantially from the boundaries of others. There is no right or wrong way to set boundaries, but clarity around them enables dialogue which can minimise polarisation and conflict.

Often when something does not "feel" right, you may not have sufficient information to articulate why, but the situation may be at odds with your personal values. When your values are not honoured, your boundaries are also often crossed.

Where are your boundaries not being honoured?

With the pressure of work intensifying, many people have continued to relax their boundary around what is an acceptable level of workload. Work-related stress and burnout are often the result of not being able to say no. Unrealistic deadlines and an incessant volume of work challenge our boundaries on an almost daily basis. Holding your boundaries is essential as a leader and requires a willingness to walk away if they are not upheld. If you do not uphold your boundaries, it results in stress and overwhelm.

In moments of uncertainty, leaders can ease the discomfort that their teams and organisations experience by articulating the certainty and thereby making people feel more secure. Clarity and open dialogue around boundaries, risks and values can minimise misunderstandings and provide comfort to those who struggle with the perceived chaos of uncertainty. The easier leaders make it for their teams to navigate uncertainty, the more quickly those teams will move forward with greater confidence.

MASTERING UNCERTAINTY

- Create some certainty in periods of uncertainty.

- Focus on the things you can influence and be flexible with those you cannot.

- Articulate your values, boundaries and beliefs and encourage others to do the same, finding alliance and understanding difference.

- Replace control and power with flexibility and creativity.

- Provide clarity and set the direction.

- Be aware of your patterns of behaviour and their impact.

- Act in service of the whole rather than in service of self.

- Trust your gut instinct.

- Be clear and consistent with your boundaries.

Before you move on to the next chapter, spend 10 minutes reflecting on the balance between certainty and uncertainty in your organisation. Consider how you can provide a framework for you and your team to deal more effectively with uncertainty.

 Download the *Leading Through Uncertainty* workbook from www.judejennison.com/uncertainty and record your reflections.

PROVOKING PERSONAL INSIGHT

How can you create more certainty for you and your team as a framework for flexibility?

Where can you provide more clarity, direction and purpose?

How do you embrace uncertainty in a way that does not add energy to the struggle but instead creates a framework for safety within which people can flex?

If we accept that uncertainty generates strong emotions, how do you equip leaders to be skilled in handling those emotions?

How do you allow yourself to have emotions in relationships with others, knowing that your emotions influence your leadership?

Where are your boundaries not being honoured?

Chapter 8

CO-SENSING AND CO-SHAPING THE FUTURE

"There is no certainty in emergence. Instead, there is fluidity, flexibility and possibility. That freaks the life out of a lot of people."

Opus suddenly kicked the stable door. Bang! He was standing in his stable next to the arena. He had his head over the door, watching intently all morning as clients led different horses. He never took his eyes off the clients and paused only to eat hay when we also stopped for a break. It often surprises clients that he shows so much commitment to being involved even though he doesn't play an active hands-on role. Horses always work as a collective, which means they look out for each other all the time. If one of them is in the arena, the others always pay attention and communicate with each other constantly, even though they may be doing something else.

Opus had been quiet all morning, and although I realised that he was watching us, the clients had been engrossed and largely unaware of his presence. As we turned to look at him, he raised his head high and kicked the stable door again two or three times. "It looks as though he wants something," I said. That was an understatement. There was nothing subtle about his communication.

I went over to him. He headbutted me, then nudged the lock on his stable door. His message was clear. He wanted to come out. I put on his head collar and opened the stable door. He came barging out in a hurry. He dragged me over to the arena, charged in like a young horse at the races and pulled me over towards the clients. He went up to Ruth (client name changed to protect confidentiality) and headbutted her on the chest. She looked at me and raised her eyebrows in astonishment.

I said, "I think he wants to work with you. Are you willing?" Ruth said yes. Since his formal retirement from the leadership work, Opus is quite challenging to lead and usually plants his feet and refuses to move with clients. He requires clarity, confidence and purpose in a leader, someone who knows exactly where they are going and communicates it, balanced with gentleness, empathy and space for him to feel he has an opinion, too. It takes an exceptionally skilled leader to balance the energy of driving results with the softness of nurturing in complete harmony. Opus is the master of fine-tuning!

Clients are often too kind and respectful towards him, and he takes advantage of that. I explain that if you want to persuade your CEO to do something, you need to be compelling. If you are too passive, too nice or too respectful, you won't be influential. You need to connect, build trust, and be assertive and clear.

Ruth led Opus round the arena, and he was relaxed and calm with her. He did everything she asked, which is highly unusual. Despite being an exceptional leader, Ruth lacked confidence in her leadership and often held back and put herself down. When she saw Opus march in with power and confidence, she knew she would need to find a different style than her usual one. Holding back and diminishing her power was not going to work here, any more than it does for Ruth at work. She set off with confidence, purpose and clarity. Opus matched her step for step. Ruth learned that when she did step up with true confidence, she was highly capable. As soon as they finished, Opus headbutted me. He was ready to go. As I took the lead rope from Ruth, he dragged me to the gate and demanded to go back to the ringside seat of his stable. He was done, and he made it clear.

Ruth was shocked. She saw how Opus commanded such respect by being clear about what he wanted. I explained that he doesn't always get exactly what he wants, but he never fails to communicate it.

Ego to eco

The desire for fast results and high achievement often leads to a focus on the end goal and prevents connection, dialogue and collaboration. We need to develop the ability to co-sense and co-shape the future as a collective, by sensing from the wider fields – including planetary, nature and physical body. This requires time and space, yet the fast pace of work is not conducive to this.

Individual heroism is no longer relevant to leadership in an interconnected global economy and society. Many organisations continue to incentivise people based on personal achievement. This encourages self-serving leaders who are egocentric and interested in personal gain. Their impact on others is of secondary importance, which results in conflict and tension between departments as people compete for personal results.

Collective leadership encourages people to act in service of a bigger picture. The focus is on taking responsibility for your personal impact, adhering to the values and integrity of the organisation, and protecting the whole. This requires a humility in leadership, a willingness to put the achievement of the whole above the success of personal gain.

A client works with Kalle to move forward together

Collective leadership requires exploration and creativity and encourages experimentation, which is often feared in business. Co-sensing integrates thoughts and feelings into what is needed in the wider field – physically, mentally and emotionally. It requires the courage to have a go, the confidence to make mistakes and the willingness to learn from the experience and try again.

A high-performance culture benefits from setting targets that encourage teamwork and collaboration, but often fails to do so. The Western approach to leadership must shift from leading from the front and being the hero in the spotlight to inspiring, engaging and working together to improve the way we live and work.

Where can you switch more from self-serving leadership to being in service of a greater good?

Slow down to speed up

Collective leadership takes more time initially to build relationships and establish the collective aims. The challenge that leaders face is to slow down the pace in order to speed up. Momentum builds when human connection and strong relationships have been developed. The slowing down is momentary, and it takes self-discipline to make space for this.

While slowing down seems counterintuitive, the faster a conversation becomes, the more confused people are and the more people struggle to keep up. When they focus on being quick enough to get their own point of view across, they prevent co-creation as they focus on what they already know and cease to listen to each other. When you slow down conversation, there is more space for dialogue, listening and curiosity. This increases understanding of others and builds relationships more quickly.

When you slow down, you have space to go beyond the known information that is available. New thoughts and ideas emerge by building on the thoughts and ideas of others, and logical connections can be made by thinking them through carefully. When you slow down, you have space to pay attention at a deeper level, which leads to the ability to respond to fast-changing environments.

Slowing down is, paradoxically, a crucial component of speeding up. We can achieve more and faster when we slow down and embrace dialogue and listening. Slowing down provides clarity on what you are thinking and feeling, enabling you to make more measured decisions by integrating the head, heart and gut. We need to give leaders the skills to slow down even when it is counterintuitive, and help them recognise the importance of reflection. Through reflection, leaders increase self-awareness and understanding, explore different ways of doing things and allow new ideas to emerge. This fosters a culture of innovation as well as connection and supports a fast-paced, high-performance culture.

A fast pace can create disconnection as people struggle to keep up. Instead they tend to veer the conversation towards what they already know and strive to get their opinion across. This prevents collaboration and does not allow for explanation and understanding.

Where are you disconnected and need to slow down?

Every time you experience disconnection, try slowing down to reconnect. It creates space to understand others at a non-verbal level, recognising the values, beliefs and drivers behind the approach of others. This increases trust and creates a level of intimacy in a team.

Case study – Richard*

Richard took Kalle's lead rope and set off down the arena. It never occurred to him to invite her to come with him. He assumed she would follow his lead. As he walked away, Kalle never moved a foot, but she turned her head sharply away from him, causing such tension in the lead rope that Richard was dragged back. He looked surprised. He was in such a hurry that it shocked him when she would not go willingly. Richard didn't make time to build a connection with Kalle, and she was going nowhere without it. I explained that she wanted to be in relationship, so he stood stroking her, but Richard's mind continued to be on the end goal of how he could get her to move and complete the task.

After Richard had spent time stroking Kalle, then trying to get her to move and failing, I asked him whether he was "doing relationship" or "being in relationship". He wasn't sure what I meant at first, then he realised. He was stroking Kalle because he thought it was a necessary step to complete the task, not because he wanted to be in relationship with her. The relationship was not congruent. The perceived connection of him stroking Kalle was another essential task that slowed down the overall goal. Once Richard realised this, he spent time with her to truly build a connection. This time she engaged with him, and off they went.

As they walked, Richard was sensing into Kalle's needs. While he had his own regular pace of doing things, Kalle was much slower, and Richard moderated his pace to encourage her to come with him. They found a joint pace that was faster than Kalle's and slower than Richard's. They were co-sensing and co-shaping. At the far end of the arena, Kalle came to a stop. Richard was not sure what she wanted, so he stopped, too.

Richard explained that he is very driven and often butts up against people whose opinion differs from his. He is known for being coercive and dominant, but he didn't know another way. Once he felt the difference between doing and being in relationship, Richard was able to start building better relationships in work, too. Although he'd repeatedly had feedback at work asking him to build better relationships, he didn't know how. He needed the experience of it working and not working so that he could recalibrate his approach and fine-tune the way he did it. Working with Kalle, he found a new way of co-creating that he had never experienced before. The hard work of constant practice happened when he returned to the workplace. He now has a new reference point for the skill of co-shaping and co-sensing, and it is transforming his relationships at work.

* Name changed to protect confidentiality

Flexibility

In a performance-driven culture, there is a tendency to go flat out in pursuit of achieving goals. Leaders need increased flexibility to allow human connection when leading through uncertainty. When we pay attention to what is needed by each member of the team as well as the overall organisation, we collaborate more effectively and lead more collectively.

A performance-driven culture often does not allow for mistakes, and this makes the environment unsafe and becomes a barrier to connection. Connection can look and feel very different to everyone, and therefore flexibility is needed to create an intentional impact in challenging environments.

Organisations that create a culture where it is safe to speak out increase creativity and innovation by allowing people to make mistakes and to take more liberties in different approaches. Most organisations have created the polar opposite to this. The culture is fast-paced, high-pressure, rife with stress, overwhelm, control, fear and polarisation, all of which prevent flexibility, a slower pace and the ability to co-create the future. In such a culture, risks are rarely reported honestly and become apparent only when they crystallise into major issues, requiring corrective action that is typically expensive and time-consuming.

Continual disruptive learning provides leaders with the skills to flex and recalibrate moment by moment. Careful consideration should be given to how organisations create an environment for continual learning so that people learn how to co-create.

Sensing from the wider field

Where do you have your best ideas? In the shower? Walking the dog? Riding your bike? Running? It's unlikely that you have them in the middle of a meeting when you are reviewing progress against key performance indicators. Ideas don't come from cognitive processing. If you've ever had a sleepless night, you'll know that you rarely solve your problem until you get up. The more you lie awake trying to work something out, the more it eludes you. You get up, have a shower, and suddenly the answer is obvious, and you wish you hadn't spent two hours in the night tossing and turning over something so simple.

The answers to many of the world's problems, on both a micro and a macro level, are within reach, but they are not in your head. Leaders who find time to switch off often find inspiration from things happening around them. Pushing and pulling does not yield results. Rather, it creates unnecessary stress and pressure and slows down innovation, creativity and, ultimately, results.

We need to rebalance how we use the left and right brain functions and tap into the wisdom of a wider system. By slowing down and being willing to be flexible, you make space to co-create with others, to sense into the wider field of wisdom.

The uncertainty of the era in which we live means that we respond to the global economic and political systems. Events in one country affect others, and changing market conditions require organisations to be more flexible. Large organisations find it more difficult to respond quickly to changing markets. Against the backdrop of economic and political uncertainty, the millennials are influencing the workplace, and so the requirements for employees are also changing.

Organisations need to flex and respond quickly to continuous change. When we pay attention to what is needed in the wider system outside, we can flex our approach and create new ways of working, as well as new products and services that meet the needs of the ever-evolving market. Companies such as Amazon have fundamentally shaped the way we shop, generating the online shopping phenomenon that we take so much for granted today. Technology provides opportunities for new businesses to spring up and quickly dominate a more traditional market. Every business needs to stay focused on external conditions and be able to adapt quickly by sensing into the external environment and making use of the information.

What information are you ignoring in the wider external environment, and how does that inform you?

Focus on looking forward is a key component of co-shaping from the external conditions. We might not be able to change the circumstances within which we are operating, but we can change our attitude and commit to finding new ways to operate.

As more companies put all their budget into online learning only, it is essential for me as a business owner to articulate the difference between e-learning and experiential learning and the value of what I bring. What sets me apart is the substantial and rapid behavioural change that I can create in leaders by working with horses. In fact, these external market conditions shape the way I communicate with clients, ensuring that I articulate my benefits clearly. By sensing into my environment as well as understanding my strengths, I can create an opportunity for more clarity with my clients by articulating how the learning with horses has value and gets results in a way that they cannot achieve online or in a classroom.

Micro vs macro

We often consider uncertainty at a macro level. We explore the uncertainty of the economic or political situation, define the strategy of an organisation, and identify the product and services that might expand or disrupt an industry or market. Many people are skilled in this.

In my interviews with numerous leaders, they were interested in strategic foresight. They explored the various scenarios that might get played out and the associated risks, developed plans to mitigate those risks, and were ready to respond according to whichever scenario occurred. This work is critical as we navigate uncertainty on a macro level, enabling businesses to consider the future and plan ahead. But despite planning and foresight, uncertainty continues. Unforeseen events will continue to affect our everyday working lives at a micro level, and we need resilience and flexibility to adapt to changing situations.

Effective leaders are always aware of operating on a micro and a macro level. It's important to balance the two, to make sense of what something means for you, your team, your organisation and the global economy and society. Too many decisions are made at the micro or macro level that have an unconscious ripple effect.

When call centres were moved to India in the 1990s and manufacturing went to China, few considered the impact on society in their decision-making process. The decisions were largely based on the desire to reduce cost. The subsequent impact was the rise of the global economy, increased education in developing countries and the world as we know it today. The Western world rarely considered the impact to the employees in the local country whose jobs would disappear, how employment would change in the Western world, how countries like India would upskill their workforce to meet the need, where the call centres would be built or the impact that would have on society.

These decisions shaped our present and our future. In making a decision, we created uncertainty without realising it. The unintended impact of offshoring was that local people in indigenous cultures were forced from their homes so that land could be used to build call centres and technology parks on a grand scale. Did anyone in those meetings consider this when they made the decisions? I highly doubt it. We can't consider what we don't see.

If we were to make those decisions again, would we make them in the same way? Being conscious of the decisions we make is a crucial part of leading through uncertainty.

At a micro level, how do you co-sense and co-shape decisions with your clients, team and organisation?

At a macro level, how do your decisions affect the global economy, society and the planet?

133

Movement

People spend huge amounts of time in meetings discussing things, providing updates, tuning out when others speak and becoming present only when it is their turn. If you sit in meetings like this, or run meetings like this, take a stand and shake it up. Everyone knows it is ineffective, yet somehow people collude and continue to play the role. This has a major impact on productivity in business. It's not leadership. It's often born out of a desire to bring people together, but if they are not co-creating, it is not effective and leads to further disconnection.

How can you encourage people in your team to co-create business results?

Meetings are invaluable when people explore new ways of working together. They provide the space for people to collaborate, to explore what is working and what is not, and ultimately to consider how to move forward together. The key word here is movement. Meetings often go around in circles, with a lack of listening and a focus on needing to be right. There is no shortage of information or opinions, but there is no forward movement.

Many people experience the frustration of analysis paralysis, where everyone has a different opinion. The lack of listening and dialogue prevents people from being understood and causes a team to be static far longer than is necessary. Someone needs to be willing to take the first step and create from it. I often see teams spend a long time planning how they are going to move a horse. What they fail to consider is that the horse has an opinion. If the team take the first step, they can adapt and change direction en route.

Movement creates movement. When teams create movement, they create momentum. Once you have started, it is easier to review and modify your approach by being flexible as you go along. Trying to reach consensus before you begin leads to over-analysis, especially in uncertainty where the answers are unknown.

Where are you static and need to move?

Planning and strategy are essential and have their place, but they are not the only thing we have in our toolkit. Overplanning often comes from a desire for certainty. Plans can be altered once they are under way. When leading through uncertainty, we need the skills to respond to unexpected events, unforeseen circumstances and sudden changes. If we do not develop the flexibility and adaptability to respond in the moment, we become static, generate more debate without listening and create analysis paralysis. If you find yourself in a heated debate that is going nowhere, or in analysis paralysis, change your approach. Movement is the impetus for co-shaping.

By contrast, when we move away *from* something, we may move for the sake of moving. If you are moving before you have all the answers, be clear what you are moving *towards*. Movement for the sake of movement can be as damaging as analysis paralysis.

Where are you moving too quickly and need time to reflect?

Movement requires leaders to take a risk, to have a go and trust that they can create in flow, before major disasters happen. Unless you work on a production line, where everything happens in a set process, work is no longer linear. Minor setbacks provide feedback that there is another way of doing things. If we pay attention to what is happening, recover quickly and trust our instincts, we can avoid many of the failures that happen. We can co-shape and co-sense in process. Flexibility and agility are therefore crucial skills to develop in order to lead through uncertainty.

MASTERING UNCERTAINTY

- Shift your focus from egocentric to ecocentric and act in service of a bigger picture.

- Encourage and reward collective results.

- Slow down to allow new ideas to emerge.

- Take time out for reflection and for increasing self-awareness.

- Be flexible and willing to modify your approach in changing situations.

- Pay attention to what is needed in the wider system – the team, the organisation and society.

- Consider the impact of your decisions on a micro and a macro level.

- Take a risk, have a go and trust that you can create in flow.

Before you move on to the next chapter, spend 10 minutes reflecting on how you can connect to a wider eco-system to co-create with others.

 Download the *Leading Through Uncertainty* workbook from www.judejennison.com/uncertainty and record your reflections.

PROVOKING PERSONAL INSIGHT

Where can you switch more from self-serving leadership to being in service of a greater good?

Where are you disconnected and need to slow down?

What information are you ignoring in the wider external environment, and how does that inform you?

At a micro level, how do you co-sense and co-shape decisions with your clients, team and organisation?

At a macro level, how do your decisions affect the global economy, society and the planet?

How can you encourage people in your team to co-create business results?

Where are you static and need to move?

Where are you moving too quickly and need time to reflect?

Chapter 9

LISTENING AND DIALOGUE

"Dialogue is a conversation where the relationship between people is just as important as the outcome, and every voice is equal and heard."

"I don't like horses and I don't like people," Jane (not her real name) said as she introduced herself to me. She was driven by results, and her experience was that people got in the way of her getting the job done. She opted to lead Kalle, an interesting choice because Kalle is all about relationship. If you don't build a relationship with her first, she won't cooperate. Why would she? Kalle wants to know that you are paying attention and listening to her needs as well as your own.

Jane approached Kalle, stretched out her hand for Kalle to sniff, then stroked her on the side of the neck. "She's so warm!"

Jane declared. It was a cold day and she'd removed her glove to stroke Kalle. She was surprised by the warmth of the horse's coat. As Jane stroked her on the neck, Kalle turned her head towards her and gently wrapped it round her in a form of hug. It wasn't just her coat that was warm.

Jane was amazed. She had never spent time building a relationship. She went straight in, expecting people to cooperate and get the job done. She was highly successful, so her focus on results had worked to a point. She set off, inviting Kalle to come with her, which she did willingly. They got halfway round the arena when Jane stopped paying attention to Kalle. Kalle was coming, so Jane ignored her and started focusing solely on completing the task. Kalle stopped instantly. The togetherness was gone. It had become a task and a process for Jane, the relationship was broken, and Kalle had disengaged. There was no reason for Kalle to want to move without the connection.

Jane went back to Kalle, stroked her on the neck and invited her to come with her again. Kalle obliged. When Jane came back to the rest of the group, she said, "I get really frustrated when people don't come with me. I just want them to do what they are supposed to do." Her drive for results had caused friction in the team as not everyone could meet her high standards or match her fast pace. Jane realised that she was not listening to her team. She was demanding results and unaware of their need to be in dialogue and to be included in the way things were done.

Once Jane realised this, she focused more on the horses in subsequent exercises. She paid attention to them, had empathy for their needs and worked with them. At the end of the day, she said, "I've changed my mind. I do like horses, and I realise I like people, too. I've just always seen them as getting in my way, but now I realise that when I listen, we can work out how we do things together. It actually reduces the pressure on me and spreads the responsibility."

Maturity to change

At the heart of co-sensing and co-shaping the future lies an openness to change and the maturity to have our view altered by the perspectives of others. This requires a deep sense of listening, far beyond the words that are being said, to sense what wants to be expressed, including the values, beliefs, desires and needs on an individual and a collective level. True listening includes empathic listening, sensing into the emotions and feelings of others and tuning into what needs to happen next. It is the remit of the unseen as much as the seen.

Dialogue requires a much deeper level of listening. It occurs when we switch our listening from our own thoughts to sensing what is happening with others, with the environment and the wider global ecosystem. This requires leaders to find a level of patience, stillness and mindfulness that is so often lacking in fast-paced change. Dialogue provides the space for people to be seen and understood, as well as to seek to understand others. It enables true collaboration, where everyone's needs are met, rather than compromise, which is often what teams create.

Listening to self

There are different ways we can listen and it starts with listening to self. This is the primary level of listening that people adopt the majority of the time. It involves being aware of yourself and your own responses. When you listen to a presentation, you listen to what is resonant for you, where you agree or disagree, and how the information relates to you. Even though you are hearing someone speak, the listening is based on gathering information to serve you. With this level of listening, you hear the facts and information that are valuable and needed, but it doesn't deepen your understanding of the other person or develop the relationship with them. This approach is appropriate when you are listening to a presentation and don't need to build rapport.

Often the focus is on the information in the head. You have a whole body which has massive wisdom that is providing information, too. Your emotions create a visceral response in the body that is a powerful source of information and guides you to making decisions that meet your needs. When you pay attention to your visceral responses, you can align the information in your head with your emotions and gut instinct and have more aligned information available from which to make decisions.

If you listen only to yourself and you fail to listen to others, it can create disconnection. For example, if you have had a challenging day and want to share it with someone, you might start by saying, "I had a really tough day today." Your friend immediately kicks in with, "Oh me too! You won't believe what happened to me…" The moment is gone. Suddenly the conversation is on them, and you have lost the opportunity to be listened to or heard. Your friend is so busy listening to themselves that they fail to listen to you and hear you. They miss the fact that you have something that you want to share. They break the relationship with you by making the conversation about them.

Where are you creating disconnection by listening to self?

Listening to others

You can improve relationships with others by listening to them at a deep level, beyond the words that are being spoken. There is so much to notice if you listen deeply and seek to understand the person and what is important for them. You can identify their values and beliefs, their wants and needs, as well as their fears, by listening beyond the words, including their energy, emotions and the impact they have on you. As you pay attention to these things, be aware of the listening to self that also happens. Notice the facts and information that you hear, and consider how they inform you about that person. Notice the stories you create and the assumptions you make. How do you feel about the person and situation, and how do you think they feel?

This form of listening takes practice as most people have never listened at such a deep level before. You have probably either listened to yourself and how things relate to you or listened to others and what is happening for them. Now it's time to integrate the two. Integrated listening builds stronger relationships through a deeper connection. It is powerful to be heard and understood in this way.

Jude takes time to deepen the relationship with Kalle and Tiffin

The ability to listen at this level is even more important (and often overlooked) when there is conflict. That is the time that you may want to focus on appeasing someone or fighting for your rights. Usually, in conflict, people pay attention to their own needs, increasing the disconnection and causing the relationship to break down further. We need to collaborate through differences of opinion and include cultural differences in the decision-making. That requires you to listen deeply to yourself and respect your opinions, views, thoughts and feelings, while also listening to others and respecting their opinions, views, thoughts and feelings, even when they may be vastly different to your own. This is true mutual respect, in which everyone's needs are met. I cover this in more detail in my book *Leadership Beyond Measure*.

By listening to and integrating the needs of everyone, you can develop solutions in harmony with others. Relationships transform when you articulate your own needs as well as truly listening to the needs of others and find ways to integrate both without compromise.

Where can you listen to others more?

Colin D. Smith, aka The Listener, works with executives and leaders to develop the subtle art of listening. He advocates that learning to listen is like going to the gym – if you expect results in the first week, you've missed the point. Learning to listen is a long-term practice that exponentially improves the way people work together.

> ❝*Listening is an art, a skill and a discipline, and therefore requires a subtle long-term approach. Learning to listen is like going to the gym. For the first few weeks of regular attendance, nothing seems to change, then you start to climb the stairs two at a time, stand taller and feel more confident. So it is with listening.*
>
> *The first step is to accept that you may not listen as well as you could, then to understand the differences between hearing and listening, the practical elements of listening, and finally to begin putting these into practice, by being a listener.*
>
> *Initially the changes seem small, and it is easy to give up on developing listening as a skill. Those who persevere rarely see listening as a big change, rather a decision that they make to develop the skill of listening, slowly and sustainably. Feedback from clients indicates*

that the impact of their listening grows exponentially as the discipline grows stronger. Their meetings become less frenetic, shorter and more engaging. Their conversations are more thoughtful, of a higher quality, go deeper, feel energising and so much more – all from simply learning to listen. The more we listen to others, the more likely they are to listen to us and the more easily we can engage in dialogue.

For one executive, it all stemmed from a simple exercise where he could both see and feel the impact of his behaviour of physically and emotionally dropping out of a conversation. He realised he had not been listening. In fact, he was barely even hearing his colleagues. He also realised the same behaviour was happening at home with his wife and their young children. He vowed at that moment to change the way he would listen to those in his team.

The first 'muscle' he developed was an intention to listen as many times as possible. He started to notice when he faced the person speaking and was fully present with them. He removed all the distractions that created disconnection – his mobile, TV, tablet, etc. He made an effort to be curious and interested. He noticed that when he started to formulate his response, he had stopped listening. He remained silent, did not interrupt, and let the person finish speaking. He became curious about what else they might say and quietly asked, "What more?"

The change in the way people responded to him was profound. They seemed happier, more engaged and more trusting. He explained that they felt heard, valued, trusted, and that they mattered. It transformed his leadership.

PWC's annual global CEO survey 2016[8] identified that "55% of CEOs are concerned about a lack of trust in business today" and that "a high level of trust makes employees more committed to staying with the company, partners are more willing to collaborate and investors more prepared to entrust stewardship of their funding".

Listening is the foundation to building trust and is cited in the 2017 Edelman Trust Barometer Report[9] as "a trust-building and operational imperative".

—Colin D. Smith, aka The Listener

Listening to the environment

Most people stop at listening to self and others, but there is more information you can include in your listening and leadership. Listening to the environment isn't limited to hearing; it involves feeling into the energy and emotion, and sensing into the atmosphere. For example, you may sense tension in a meeting where there are disagreements or conflict. Or you may notice the temperature in a room and observe that a warm room causes the energy of the people in the room to dip. You may also notice when some people disconnect in moments of tension while others engage more forcefully to have their voice heard. This

---

[8] PWC, Annual CEO Survey: Redefining business success in a changing world, 2016. Available from: www.pwc.com/gx/en/ceo-survey/2016/landing-page/pwc-19th-annual-global-ceo-survey.pdf [accessed 18 March 2018].

[9] Edelman Trust Barometer Report 2017. Available from: www. scribd.com/document/336621519/2017-Edelman-Trust-Barometer-Executive-Summary#fullscreen&from_embed [accessed 18 March 2018].

affects the mood of the room and can provide information on what is needed to create a positive outcome for the overall team and for the collective goals and objectives.

At this level of listening, you can see who is engaged and disengaged and how to bring the whole team together.

> *As a leader, your role is to notice what needs to happen next. What is the powerful leadership action that you can take based on all the information you have – by listening to self, to others and to the environment?*

Does someone need to be invited to share their opinion and be given the space to do so? How can you create a safe space for that to happen?

What information in the environment are you ignoring?

In any group, there will be different opinions or voices. Pay attention to those who don't speak up. They may be afraid to speak to something that they feel is not likely to be well received, or they may negate their opinion by believing they are the only one who thinks or feels that way. Every voice in the system is important. Often we hold back from having difficult conversations in order to avoid conflict, yet the situation has an impact even when it is unspoken. By listening to what is truly going on beyond the words, you can voice what is happening and create an environment of openness and transparency.

What needs to be voiced in your system?

Horses invite us to pay attention at this level. As herd animals whose safety is constantly under threat from predators, horses have learned to pay attention to the environment. They miss nothing. Every fox that appears, every leaf that blows in the wind could have an impact on their safety. Horses are often considered unpredictable by humans who don't afford the same level of listening to the environment. If you've ever been surprised by something that you didn't see coming, it may be because you were not paying attention to the bigger picture. If you miss the subtle signs, you'll constantly be surprised by things that happen or by things people say and do. We need to continually switch our attention between listening to self, others and the environment.

Working with horses enables people to develop this skill quickly, to recognise that the wider system is impacting the horse as well as their leadership, and to include it in the conversation. Once you have learned the importance of focusing on the task, the facts and the information, your internal dialogue, the relationship and the environment, you can start to balance how you listen in the workplace and how you include all elements of information.

Task vs relationship

When people work with the horses, the balance between task and relationship becomes obvious very quickly. Some clients focus on achieving the task and getting the horse round the arena and back to where they started as quickly as possible. They may feel nervous and rush to get it over and done with. If you focus too much on the task, you break the relationship and lose sight of the bigger picture and what is happening around you. In these moments the horses usually plant their feet and refuse to move, or they may go with you and take charge along the way, either stopping or veering off or dragging you round quickly.

Other clients are so focused on the relationship that they forget where they are going. The horses are willing to engage because they feel respected and trusted, but in the absence of a clear direction, again they will either plant their feet or drag you around. In the process you lose sight of your needs. In your desire to be in relationship, you give the power over to the other party, and suddenly you realise that you have not achieved what you wanted to achieve. This is what happens to people pleasers.

In a bid to get everyone's buy-in, they focus too much on what other people want and forget about their own needs.

Sometimes clients are able to balance their own needs with the needs of others by listening to both, and the horse follows willingly. Sometimes clients say, "I was so focused that I had no idea what was happening around me."

They become so focused on the task and the relationship and suddenly notice that the rest of the team are heading in a different direction or not moving at all. If you've ever experienced things occurring out of the blue, you've failed to notice that the environment has changed. As a result of a new boss, the culture evolves and the requirements change, but if you're focused purely on the relationship with others, you'll miss it. If you've ever found yourself putting your head down and doing an outstanding job only to find that someone else has got a promotion or a pay rise that you think you should have got, then you might want to lift your head and start paying more attention to what is going on around you.

Self. Others. Environment. Deep listening involves paying attention to all three all at the same time and making powerful leadership choices based on the information from the head, heart and gut.

Values, needs and beliefs

Deep listening enables you to sense the values, needs and beliefs of other people, behind the words that are said. You can also gain insight into the emotions and feelings of others when you pay attention at this level.

Values and beliefs shape the thoughts, feelings and actions of others, so the more you understand their mode of operation, the easier it is to work through differences. What's important to one person will be different from what's important to another. Some people have a value around work–life balance, where others have a value around working hard. Of course, those two values can go hand in hand, but they don't always. That's why listening is essential at a deeper level because we often use words that we think we understand when in fact we mean a completely different thing.

Misunderstandings arise from poor communication, not just in articulating what we want but in listening to what is needed and paying attention to people's levels of understanding.

What values are you not honouring in yourself?

What values are others trying to communicate?

At an organisational level, many companies have recognised the need for company values. Few have created an environment where those values come alive. In addition, everyone will have a different perspective on the application and implication of the company values. For example, trust is something that everyone thinks they are good at, yet few people truly trust themselves fully or others when leading through uncertainty.

Space for dialogue

Dialogue can occur only when we are willing to listen at a deeper level as well as at a wider level (the environment). In dialogue, we notice our differences as well as our similarities. People are naturally drawn to others like themselves, which means we navigate towards those who agree with us. If you focus on listening to self, you will find yourself surrounded by people who think like you and behave like you because they will validate your thoughts and opinions. That's fundamentally bad for business as it stifles creativity, as well as excluding minority groups. While it is important to stand up for your values, rights and beliefs, it is essential that you also make space for others' values, rights and beliefs. We need to hold the paradox of "both/and" rather than "either/or" and act in service of the whole instead of acting in service of our own rights at the expense of others.

Dialogue involves being in relationship with people who may have different opinions, and exploring new approaches together. Companies that encourage diverse teams are more innovative and have higher market growth. Innovation occurs when everyone is heard and feels safe to propose new ideas, without blame, judgement or criticism.

The point of dialogue is not to analyse things, win over others or have your opinion validated. Dialogue provides an opportunity for people to come together and create new ideas, giving and listening to feedback, taking on board objections and finding new ways around them. Dialogue requires us to put aside the need to win, to have our opinion validated or discounted.

> *Dialogue can occur only when we have learned to listen. It lifts us out of polarisation and into alignment for the sake of creating something new. It is a conversation in which the relationship between people is as important as the outcome, where every voice is equal and heard.*

Dialogue can be effortless and flowing, born out of the foundation of curiosity, openness and flexibility. It can also be challenging when we are faced with diverse and polarised opinions. It requires a presence and a stillness to truly listen at a deeper level and a dance of thoughts and feelings bouncing around to create something new. Curiosity leads to a new discovery, enabling ideas to be expressed and built upon.

Where might dialogue improve your relationships?

We often believe we are in dialogue when in fact we are merely expressing opinions to each other without fully appreciating each other's needs. Dialogue is an advanced form of communication that can transform teams and enhance relationships.

MASTERING UNCERTAINTY

- Be willing to change and have the maturity to have your view altered by the perspectives of others.

- Listen to self to gather facts and information that affect you.

- Listen to others to understand how they operate and be curious about their values and beliefs.

- Provide time for dialogue and understanding so that people feel heard and understood.

- Pay attention to the emotional field and use its wisdom as information.

- Prevent and resolve misunderstandings by articulating your needs clearly.

- Focus on the task and the relationship in equal measure.

- Be curious where there is misunderstanding and let go of needing to be right or validated.

Before you move on to the next chapter, spend 10 minutes reflecting on how well you listen and where you could improve the quality of the dialogue.

 Download the *Leading Through Uncertainty* workbook from www.judejennison.com/uncertainty and record your reflections.

PROVOKING PERSONAL INSIGHT

Where are you creating disconnection by listening to self?

Where can you listen to others more?

What information in the environment are you ignoring?

What needs to be voiced in your system?

What values are you not honouring in yourself?

What values are others trying to communicate?

Where might dialogue improve your relationships?

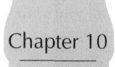

Chapter 10

CONNECTION AND SUPPORT

"Moments of deep connection are fleeting. In that instant, you feel the vulnerability of being seen, understood and known."

The group and I stood at the gate to the field, and I introduced the horses who were grazing. I turned to Kalle, and she lifted her head and looked at us. I moved on to talk about Tiffin, and Kalle went back to her grazing. As I mentioned Tiffin's name, he also lifted his head and took a step forward towards us. I turned to look at Gio and before I even mentioned his name, he walked over to the gate to meet everyone.

On this particular day, Mr Blue was in a stable waiting for the vet to come and perform minor surgery on his foot. I explained that he would not be part of the day but that he might at some point pop his head out of the stable to say hello. At that moment, as if by magic, his face appeared over the stable door. Meanwhile, Opus, my 29-year-old retired horse, was 50 metres away in a small paddock standing behind a 5 ft bale of hay, eating. You could just about see him. The gate to the paddock was open as Opus has the full run of the yard when I am onsite – it's his privilege as the old man of the herd.

As I started to explain about Opus being retired, he looked up and stepped to one side of the hay bale so we could see him. One of the clients gasped, "Does he really know you are talking about him? Have you trained them to do this?" Yes, they know when we are talking about them, and no, I have not trained them. In fact, it's the opposite. All of my horses are encouraged to be themselves, to be as close to a natural horse as is possible in a domesticated environment, to have an opinion and to assert their right to make it clear. It sounds incredible but this is a pattern that plays out repeatedly when introducing clients to the horses.

We continued our conversation, and I explained that Opus had free run of the yard and would probably want to come and meet them at some point throughout the day. At that moment, Opus walked out of the field and up the yard towards us. He stopped halfway and stood sentinel outside the gate to the arena. We were heading there next, and he knew it.

We walked down the yard to enter the arena, and Opus blocked our path. He stood quietly, commanding respect and attention. As each client walked past him, they said hello to him. Some of them stroked his neck, others let him sniff their hand. They were completely in awe of what had just happened. Once each person had said hello to Opus, he relaxed further and let them pass. When one person tried to pass him without greeting, he stretched out his neck and blocked their way until they said hello. There was no doubt who was in charge in this moment, and the connection was felt deeply by everyone.

People are often surprised by my relationship with the horses. They comment on how connected we are and how much respect

I give each of them. The horses are allowed to have their opinion, and I work with them without using force, which is rare in any walk of life. As soon as we revert to force, we have ceased to lead. I invite the horses to want to work with me and my clients. As a result, their level of engagement is high.

Connecting in different ways

Connection looks and feels different to everyone. Some people feel connected only when they are physically in the same location while others feel connected at a distance and out of sight. Opus is formally retired from working with clients as he found it too tiring. He typically spends the day out in the field when I work with clients. Despite that, he is always connected to me and always pays attention. If I mention his name, he will lift his head and start to walk towards the gate. This always surprises clients. They ask whether he hears me mention his name when he is at least 50 metres away. He doesn't, but he senses when he is being spoken about, just as you sense it in the office, too. This is the power of connection. We are energetically connected far more than we may realise.

Each of the horses connects in very different ways. Kalle often connects in a maternal and nurturing way when she senses someone needs to be supported. By contrast, she will headbutt you into next week if she thinks you need to be put in your place! Both are forms of connection, providing feedback in different ways according to what she senses you need. There is no self-serving leadership here. She is leading in service of the whole. Opus connects by being around us, by missing nothing and coming when he is spoken about. He will strut down the yard, ignoring everyone. Contrary to Kalle's way of connecting, he shows no tenderness in these moments; instead he commands respect and reverence for his elder wisdom. The connection is no less deep, even if he is not gazing deeply into your eye in a loving way!

Every leader has a different way of connecting. When you know what your default pattern is, you can see the impact you have on different people and flex your style according to what is required. Connection is a two-way process, and not everyone wants to connect in the same way. If someone rejects the connection, it is not necessarily a personal affront but rather a difference to be curious about, understood and embraced.

How do your team members connect with you and each other?

Opposites often attract, so everyone will find it easier or more difficult to connect with different people. The challenge as leaders is to foster an environment where everyone feels safe to connect in their own way, by bringing all of themselves.

When clients experience the depth of connection they get with the horses, they feel the power and also the vulnerability of being in connection. Once they have experienced connection in this way, they are less afraid of it and return to the workplace knowing how to connect in a variety of ways according to different needs.

Building rapport

The moment many clients feel connected to the horses is when they have their first interaction with them. Even observing the horses in the field at the beginning of the day, clients may feel disconnected and merely passive observers. The same is not true for the horses. The split second clients walk through the gate, the horses have a sense of who the clients are, their energy, intentions, emotions and sensitivity. The clients have entered their territory. The safety and integrity of the herd are in question, and the horses need to be aware of that and assess it.

In these first few moments, before clients have even realised it, they have created an impact. The same is true with people. You may not be consciously aware, but subconsciously you assess everyone you meet before you shake their hand. You already have a sense of whether you want to be connected or not. You feel drawn or repelled based on their energy.

How do **you** *show up in the first moment of connection?*

Most clients arrive feeling nervous. This can vary from being mildly nervous at being out of their comfort zone, terrified at the prospect of doing something different, or slightly unsure how it will pan out. People handle their nerves differently. Some arrive posturing and pretending that everything is fine. There may be high levels of banter and humour that mask the discomfort and distract them from feeling what they really feel. Others are more open and transparent about their feelings, naming the anxiety or discomfort early on. As one person names it, the others relax and open up, too. Being honest, transparent and vulnerable in this way is a huge strength as it opens the doorway for others to connect human to human, without all the self-imposed expectations of how they think they should be.

Respect, trust and connection can all be established in an instant. Of course, they deepen over time as well. How you show up in that first moment of connection has an impact. How you feel influences that connection, too.

What impact do you create and is it what you want?

Our capacity to connect is amazing and heart-warming, and is limited only by our attention, belief and fear.

Deepening connection

Moments of deep connection are fleeting. In that moment, there is a feeling of being seen, understood and known. It is vulnerable to be seen at that level, which is why we connect and disconnect, on and off.

When clients meet the horses, they often look them in the eye. The horses draw you in as far as you are willing to go. The connection can be deep. Some horses draw you in further than others. It depends on how they feel towards you as well as how you feel about them. Once you have built a deep level of connection, however fleeting, it becomes easier to align through differences. When you truly see someone as a human being, there is an opportunity to meet them in that humanity. When we are in conflict, we are more likely to objectify people, which leads to disconnection.

Clients regularly tell me that it takes months to build trust. When they hold this as a core belief, they prevent connection with others. They often explain that they drop their guard more with their team and connect with them more deeply than with other departments within the organisation. They allow people they know to see them. By contrast, other departments are regarded as the competition or even the enemy, competing for resources, making unreasonable requests, creating more workload and generating conflict. Co-sensing and co-shaping are missing from these relationships. Continually building connection takes time and effort and may depend on how important the relationship is. Connection creates an intimacy and a vulnerability of being seen at a deep level, which people often shy away from.

When clients work with me and the horses, they quickly establish trust and connection. While I am more forgiving and able to stay connected when clients disconnect, the horses will refuse to engage unless trust and connection are established first. In this way, clients learn to connect and trust quickly and reframe their story around how long it takes to build.

Many people are running at such high speed, they have become disconnected from themselves. Your body is not just a carrier for the brain or the machine that gets you from A to B. You are your body as well as your mind. Your body provides information about stresses and strains, it is your life force, your sense of being in the world. It is only when you can truly connect to yourself that you can create connection with others. The horses invite us to pay more attention to our physical bodies, to be aware of where we are in relation to them and each other, and to pay attention to the gut instinct and emotions that are invoked in their presence.

Alignment

It is important to stay connected through differences of opinion. There is a tendency to withdraw from people you disagree with as a form of self-protection. With increased pressure, the tension between individuals and/or departments grows. People focus on their own needs because they do not have the bandwidth to support others. The overall company strategy and vision can often seem far removed from the day-to-day actions, and competing targets and objectives create further tension.

How do you align with other departments to meet the needs of everyone?

When we make work more meaningful, people stay engaged. It is easier to align around common goals and to iron out differences along the way when we work towards a common vision or purpose.

Where are you not aligned and how can you create that alignment?

People think they are aligned but often use the same language to mean different things. Tension is created when people do not deliver as you would expect them to deliver, often based on misunderstandings over what appear to be obvious things. Be open and curious, take time to listen, and engage in dialogue to rebuild connection.

Laurel Dines, HR Director for Hudson Talent Solutions, was amazed by how quickly the horses responded to what people were thinking and feeling. She discovered key insights that she has been able to take back to the boardroom to improve the way the team connect.

> "There were four of us trying to lead a horse around an obstacle course, something you would think was really simple. However, although we knew what we wanted to do and had in part discussed tactics, it soon became very clear that we all had different ideas of how to do it. When the horse did not respond, it was frustrating. We thought we were agreed and had a shared purpose, but we were disjointed in our approach and this confused the horse to the state of inaction. Once the horse stopped, getting back on track was really difficult.
>
> It brought home to me how often this lack of alignment happens in the workplace and why we are then surprised and frustrated that nothing changes. We look for excuses – "it's them, not us" – but direct feedback from a horse is unavoidable. It's not offensive, it's just fact, and you have to change your approach or nothing happens.
>
> I've been on umpteen team-building events, but this was different. This beautiful horse is just standing, refusing to move until you get aligned as a team. That feeling when you ask the horse to come with you, and they do, is magical. It really brought home that this is how we need to work with people in the workplace as well. It's so powerful.
>
> When we go at 120 mph, we don't spend enough time building the connection with people. We need to slow down, make time to connect and build the relationship, otherwise everything suffers.

—Laurel Dines, HR Director, Hudson Talent Solutions

Remote connections

Leading virtual teams brings a greater challenge of connection. People feel more comfortable looking someone in the eye. There is a sense of knowing. Without the visual clues, you need to rely on other senses. Leading virtual teams brings about the uncertainty of connection. It requires greater trust in others. When you speak to people on a conference call, you know who has switched off. You sense it energetically if everyone is disengaged. Connection is a felt sense, and you do not need to physically see it.

A client creates a connection with Kalle

When you trust your instincts and intuition about who is not engaged, you can be curious and engage in dialogue around what is causing the disconnection. Many conference calls are an excuse to get everyone together to provide updates, but if people have timed out, there is no value. We can find new ways to build connection within a team without creating the disconnection of update calls where nobody listens and everyone disconnects. Technology can hinder or support you in this, and how you use it is a leadership choice moment by moment.

What calls are you leading that have no value to the whole team?

How can you encourage remote team working that deepens the connection?

Network and community

Our communities look very different today from how they did in the 20th century. Local communities have become global. We rely on technology to connect us, but human connection is what really creates community. Build your own communities of different people so that you are supported in times of uncertainty, according to what you need in any given moment. These communities can be virtual and/or local. Find a combination that supports your need for support and connection.

Most people have no idea that their colleagues support them. They never ask for help because they believe it will lead to them being disrespected. Instead they struggle on, not knowing how to do something, feeling more and more under pressure to perform and to create results when nothing is certain. There is a need to move from blame, judgement and criticism to a culture of support. More collaborative ways of working can ensure everyone gets support from each other to navigate their challenges.

Formal mentoring programmes can be enormously helpful, and informal ones can be just as useful. I have numerous informal mentors who I talk to when I get stuck. I rarely need to push through on my own. Just being listened to and sharing your challenge is helpful because you gain clarity by giving voice to the issue. It moves from a jumble in your head to a clear problem that can be worked on, with support from others who are less emotionally charged around the issue.

Uncertainty is challenging and uncomfortable, and there are no prizes for being a hero and going it alone. The most common thing I hear CEOs, MDs and executives say is how lonely they are at the top. They feel unsupported, yet they need only to ask for help or advice and people will provide support.

Giving voice to a problem can remove the emotional charge from it, as long as it is done in a compassionate way. When you express righteous indignation, you release dopamine into your system, which gives you an initial good feeling. This is an addictive hormone, which means you are likely to repeat the same frustration over and over. Organisations can quickly build up a culture where people complain with no intention of taking responsibility for doing anything about it. This leads to constant negativity. Notice where you are expressing righteous indignation. You have a choice over how you want to respond. You can either ignore the situation (in which case drop the moaning) or decide what action you want to take, finding support as you do so.

Most people believe that they are being criticised by others. In believing this, they create the energetic environment for criticism. When you reach out to others for support, they usually want to help. If people are stretched, they may not be able to help every time, but it does not mean they are not willing. Everyone is under pressure. Give people a chance to provide support and be mutually supported. Recognise also when they cannot and do not take it personally.

We need to shift from a culture of disconnection and discomfort to one of connection, relationship and community. This requires a willingness to be truly seen and to trust that whatever happens in uncertainty, we can navigate it together. After all, our ability to come together when needed is the core of our humanity. If we can come together in moments of crisis, we can connect on an every day basis too. Business will be all the better for it and so will the human race.

MASTERING UNCERTAINTY

- Explore how others connect in different ways.

- Foster an environment where everyone feels safe to connect in their own way, by bringing all of themselves.

- Notice where you use technology to distract or disconnect.

- Build trust, respect and connection quickly before focusing on the task.

- Notice where others disconnect and invite them to re-engage.

- Stay connected through differences of opinion and avoid the need to withdraw for self-protection.

- Clarify what you mean and understand to ensure alignment.

- Slow down and take time to connect and build relationships.

Before you move on to the next chapter, spend 10 minutes reflecting on how you connect with others and where you could deepen the relationship to support others better.

 Download the *Leading Through Uncertainty* workbook from www.judejennison.com/uncertainty and record your reflections.

PROVOKING PERSONAL INSIGHT

How do your team members connect with you and each other?

How do you show up in the first moment of connection?

What impact do you create and is it what you want?

How do you align with other departments to meet the needs of everyone?

Where are you not aligned and how can you create that alignment?

What calls are you leading that have no value to the whole team?

How can you encourage remote team working that deepens the connection?

Chapter 11

BUILDING TRUST

*"You can build trust in an instant,
and you can break it in an instant, too.
Trust is a leadership choice."*

Gio walked calmly off the horse lorry and stood with his head held high, surveying the environment. How would he integrate with the rest of the herd? It was uncertain – both for him and me. I badly wanted him to integrate without a hitch. There was a lot riding on this moment!

As a prey animal, it is stressful for horses to move to a new yard. Their safety depends on their ability to integrate into the herd. I had no reference for how Gio would behave. He walked calmly off the lorry, trusting me and trusting himself. He was vulnerable. He could have panicked and tried to retreat, but that would have rendered him less safe. It may be counterintuitive, but Gio created his safety through trust and vulnerability.

His sense of calm as he stepped off the lorry helped me to trust him in return. We built mutual trust in that instant, as I realised he would not throw his 700 kg of weight about. I also trusted in my horsemanship and leadership capabilities. I knew that I could handle him if he panicked. My calm sense of trust provided an environment for Gio to relax into. We co-created trust, both being vulnerable in the process.

Tiffin and Kalle stood in the field at the end of the paddock watching from the other side of the gate. Gio sensed he needed to win them over. He walked calmly and confidently down the paddock towards them, past Mr Blue and Opus on the other side of the fence. Tiffin grew as tall as he could as Gio approached. I was thankful the gate was between them as I watched to see what would happen. Gio walked over to Tiffin at the gate and dropped his head to the floor to show he was no threat. He was building trust and respect. Tiffin stood still, taken aback. He had been ready for a fight. He dropped his head to the floor as well and they sniffed each other through the gate. The first meeting had gone well, albeit with the safety of separate paddocks.

Three days later, I stood watching the horses. It was a scorching hot day. With the sun beating down, all of the horses were dozing calmly with their eyes half-closed. Was it too soon to integrate Gio into the rest of the herd?

The previous horse to arrive on my yard had not integrated well. He had been dominant and aggressive in the herd as well as with my human team, and he had left the yard a year later, leaving everyone exhausted. It had been a challenging process that created stress for me and my team (horse and human). Now here was Gio attempting to integrate. I desperately didn't want to put my equine herd or human team through a similar experience. I had a choice – to trust that Gio was different or to be anxious about his integration into the herd. I chose to trust him.

Trust is a leadership choice

I opened the gate, feeling slightly nervous. I didn't want anyone to be injured. I had to trust that Gio would show sensitivity to the herd, trust that the rest of the herd would not hurt him, and trust that if I needed to separate him again, I could step into the herd and do that safely. By being calm and trusting Gio, I created an environment for him to relax further.

Gio was skilful in how he moved towards the herd and moved away again when he felt he was too close. He sensed into what the herd needed, continuing to edge nearer over the coming days until within a week he was fully integrated. There was no ego, no jostling for position, just a continuous ebb and flow of movement as he gradually built a foundation of trust and became a valued member of the herd.

Choosing trust

Trust is a leadership choice. There is a long-held myth that trust can take months to build. It starts from the moment you trust yourself and your leadership capabilities. Only then can you trust others.

When you start a new job in a new company, you are out of your comfort zone and your body becomes more alert as you work out how to manage your safety in a new environment. Who can you trust? Who will help you? How can you show your capabilities and be true to yourself? Is it ok to be vulnerable? When we lead through uncertainty, these are the questions that subconsciously determine our behaviour. We make decisions and choices based on the limited available information. Logic, cognitive processing and reasoning don't really help here. It ultimately comes down to self-confidence and self-belief in your abilities.

Self-awareness is a crucial part of trusting yourself. If you know what your leadership qualities are, you can stand strongly in your position, no matter how much uncertainty there is. You can count on yourself for those qualities. I know for certain that I act with courage and compassion. These are two qualities that are unquestioningly inherent in my leadership, regardless of the situation. It means that in moments of uncertainty and doubt, I have some certainty about my leadership because I trust in my ability to be courageous and compassionate in every given moment. They form part of my framework in uncertainty.

Which qualities are inherent in your leadership?

> *There is no certainty with trust. It is something you feel. You have to take a leap of faith to trust someone, but somebody has to take that first step. We can choose to trust when we have self-confidence in our abilities.*

Trust is more difficult during uncertainty. The desire to be safe and secure determines behaviour, and we often seek to protect ourselves. As a species, we are not likely to be at risk of being eaten by a tiger, but our primal responses cause us to behave in uncertainty as if we were. Everything seems to threaten our safety. Trust is an unquestioning assumption that we can create our safety. It is often focused on external interactions but it starts with self. Leaders who trust themselves first feel more confident in creating trust with others.

Where are you not trusting yourself?

Who else are you not trusting?

When clients arrive at my stables, they are nervous, unsure whether they can lead a horse and terrified of making a fool of themselves. The uncertainty they feel is immense. In the first few moments of the day, I establish trust with them. As a leader, I take responsibility for helping people who feel vulnerable to feel at ease. I am open and transparent, which helps them trust me quickly. I put aside my own vulnerability and trust that clients will get great learning, even the ones who seem highly resistant and vocal about it at the beginning. I trust that I can provide a

Tiffin and the client feel vulnerable on first meeting

great experience for them. Every action I take is based on these assumptions of trust, which means I act with integrity and do my best work. I trust my clients because I trust myself, which helps them trust me. It starts with me making that choice – to trust or not. And it is just that – a choice.

I'm transparent about the fact that my leadership is also under the spotlight. It's not a given that the horses will move for me. My leadership has to be compelling, too. When clients hear this, they are surprised but they realise we are in it together. I'm walking alongside them willing to be equally vulnerable and to learn in the process.

This sets the tone for the day. When I role model trust and vulnerability with ease, it gives permission for my clients to do the same. They establish trust with the horses in seconds in their first interaction with them, despite being scared. The horses will not go with people if they do not have trust as a basis for the relationship. The moment a client stops trusting the horse, the horse stops and refuses to move. The horse will wait until trust is re-established and as soon as it is, the horse willingly re-engages.

Trust is essential in fast-paced, high-performance cultures as it is the foundation for all relationships. Although trust is created initially through choice, it is enhanced through listening, dialogue and connection.

> *A paradigm shift is needed to foster trust in self and others, to let go of the old and allow the new to emerge. The moment we seek control, we have ceased to trust.*

How can you support your team to foster trust in uncertainty?

Being vulnerable

We look for certainty to maintain our security. When there is uncertainty, there is vulnerability. Trust requires a level of intimacy that is vulnerable for people who are used to operating behind a mask. Intimacy requires openness, transparency and honesty so that relationships can be built. When you trust yourself enough to be vulnerable, you can drop the mask and create trust with others.

One of the reasons people fear public speaking so much is because it makes them vulnerable, and they lack trust in their ability to engage an audience. They fear getting it wrong, being judged, forgetting the key messages, not being believed and not being credible. All of this is the fear of uncertainty and the associated vulnerability. There is little that is certain when you stand up to present to a group of people. Yet the more people do it, the easier it gets. It becomes part of their comfort zone and they learn to trust that they are capable.

People navigate change in different ways. A performance-driven culture creates rapid change that requires flexibility and adaptability out of the comfort zone. Many leaders are comfortable within the known environment but feel less grounded and less confident when operating in the unknown.

That's often because they don't have self-awareness and confidence in their leadership capabilities. Leadership happens out of the comfort zone in those moments when you don't know what to think, say or do.

The fear of vulnerability creates a desire to hang on to what is known, often leading to resistance. Alternatively, it causes us to drive something to conclusion quickly so that the answer is understood. Either way, we are attached to being safe, secure and certain. When leaders let go of control and step into their vulnerability in a grounded way, they create space for new experiences, ideas and opportunities to emerge. Innovation and creativity therefore require a culture of trust and letting go of control in order for people to feel safe to try something new. Innovation thrives in an environment where failure is recognised as part of the process of continual learning and people are encouraged to recover quickly and try again.

Where are you resisting letting go of control and embracing vulnerability?

With so much fear, it's no surprise that people become disconnected from their true feelings as a coping mechanism for dealing with stress. Shutting down emotions under stress enables people to function in an almost robotic and disconnected way. With the disconnection from emotions comes a disconnection from others. A fear of vulnerability often causes us to disconnect to protect ourselves and reduce the vulnerability.

Often this disconnection breaks trust; however, we can still trust through disconnection. When you disconnect, trust that it is momentary while you regain your strength to re-engage. When others disconnect, trust that it is not a personal affront towards you; rather, it is their version of self-protection while they work out how to come back. If you trust that people will work things through in their own way, you maintain open channels of communication that speed up the process of them re-engaging and reconnecting.

We can still trust when we hold polarised views – it does not mean that the relationship is broken. When you show others that you trust them in such moments, you create safety for them to return to. Trust is not a one-off activity. It requires a continuous focus to keep rebuilding and deepening relationships.

Where are you disconnecting and what is the impact?

Creating mistrust

If trust is a choice to step into our vulnerability, we can just as easily create a lack of trust by refusing to be open and vulnerable. A lack of trust is linked to fear – the fear of being hurt, getting things wrong, not being believed or not being good enough. Fear is rife during times of uncertainty and indicates a lack of trust in your own leadership capabilities. If you fail to trust yourself, your approach will be more tentative. When you trust yourself in uncertainty, you create your security by increasing your flexibility and being willing to respond to whatever shows up.

The fear we have in uncertainty is due to a lack of trust in our ability to lead. In a desire to protect ourselves, we build barriers and hide behind masks of how we want others to see us. In doing so, we create disconnection that further erodes trust.

It's a myth that trust can take weeks and months to build. It grows deeper over time, but it is a choice moment by moment.

Clients often tell me that they don't trust someone because the other person does not trust them. They've reached stalemate. Each one is waiting for the other to trust first. Someone has to break the downward spiral of mistrust. If you can hold the belief that people are inherently good, you can trust that everyone is doing their best. The media would have us believe otherwise, continuously sharing negative stories that cause people to lack trust in politicians, other countries, large corporations and our neighbours. In parallel, people are doing great work, building communities and enhancing the lives of others. Once again, it is a choice – to believe people are inherently good and trust them or to believe the opposite.

Case study – Robert*

Robert explained that he took a long time to trust people, build relationships and let his guard down.

I asked, "Do you trust me?"

"Yes," he replied. He had been onsite for about 30 minutes.

He chose to lead Tiffin, a horse who also finds it difficult to trust. Robert took the lead rope and invited Tiffin to go with him. Tiffin followed instantly, completely relaxed. When Robert returned, I asked him whether he trusted Tiffin, and he said he did. He looked surprised. He had just busted his old story that trust takes months to build. Robert's willingness to be vulnerable allowed him to build instant trust. He realised that believing trust took months to build was an old story that shaped the way he approached people at the beginning. Once Robert had reframed his story to say that trust can be built in an instant, he began to drop the masks more and more. He trusted that he could be more honest and transparent with people he didn't know, and he created trust quicker.

* Name changed to protect confidentiality

Often trust is broken when someone does not behave as you would expect them to. Many people do not seek to rebuild trust once it is broken and that has a catastrophic effect on teams and organisations. We can choose to trust people, even when we don't like their behaviour. By being curious and seeking to understand, trust can be regained, but it requires skill and courage to do this.

Where is trust broken and how can you rebuild it?

Why do we fail to rebuild trust when it is broken? Fear and self-protection. By holding back on trust, we try to create a barrier of protection, when in fact we make ourselves less safe and secure because the relationship is broken. It is the responsibility of every leader to create trust through open dialogue, connection and clarity.

Trust is often broken when another person steps over your values, boundaries or beliefs. Often this is done unknowingly, or at least because the other person's values, beliefs and boundaries are different from yours. You can choose to allow trust to remain broken in these moments, or you can engage in open dialogue and be clear about your needs and how this impacts you. When we fail to communicate our needs, we cause further mistrust and miscommunication. Opening the lines of communication without blame and judgement can transform relationships and rebuild trust.

A lack of alignment around common goals can create an unsafe environment, which erodes trust. If we don't have a voice or feel trusted, the environment within which we work feels very unsafe. This increases fear and overwhelm. Trust and transparency are therefore crucial when leading through uncertainty.

MASTERING UNCERTAINTY

- Choose trust as a starting point for every interaction.

- Use vulnerability as a strength to create trust and build relationships.

- Build trust with an open heart, an open mind, honesty and transparency.

- Be aware of when you hold back or put up a barrier as a result of a lack of trust.

- Notice how fear causes mistrust and allow yourself to be vulnerable.

- Choose to trust people even when you don't like their behaviour.

- Notice what happens to trust when others disconnect.

- Be curious about the values, boundaries and beliefs of others when trust is broken and explore the differences openly.

Before you move on to the next chapter, spend 10 minutes reflecting on the levels of trust in yourself, your team and your organisation. Reflect on how this impacts your behaviour and interactions with others.

 Download the *Leading Through Uncertainty* workbook from www.judejennison.com/uncertainty and record your reflections.

PROVOKING PERSONAL INSIGHT

Which qualities are inherent in your leadership?

Where are you not trusting yourself?

Who else are you not trusting?

How can you support your team to foster trust in uncertainty?

Where are you resisting letting go of control and embracing vulnerability?

Where are you disconnecting and what is the impact?

Where is trust broken and how can you rebuild it?

Chapter 12

STAYING WITH THE DISCOMFORT OF UNCERTAINTY

"If you stay long enough in the discomfort of uncertainty, you create transformation and breakthrough."

Kalle came flying out of the stable, snorting in fear, her head held high. I struggled to lead her. She was dancing on her toes beside me, wanting to rush off ahead but paying attention to me as well and not wanting to hurt me.

This was the afternoon session of my first workshop with clients. I was leading through uncertainty, unsure how to lead Kalle, unsure whether my workshop would work, unsure whether the clients would enjoy it. Unknowns and uncertainty in full swing. The morning had gone well. Kalle was proving to be exceptional in her first day of work, and I felt good about the learning the clients were getting. I relaxed as things were going well. As I led Kalle out, my heart rate rocketed as she bounced from foot to foot beside me.

The clients had just built an obstacle course around which they were going to lead Kalle. I was struggling to hold her, so I explained to the clients that she felt a bit unsafe and that I would let her loose in the arena first to burn off steam. I removed her head collar, and Kalle shot off. She ran up and down the arena at a flat-out gallop, snorting and looking out into the distance across the fields.

The clients looked at me as though I would know what to do. I felt uncomfortable. Nothing prepares you for moments like these. All you can do in moments of uncertainty is be curious and trust in your leadership. We stood having a conversation about how we are never in control and the importance of surrendering to what is presented and working with it.

Suddenly I heard the sound of a hunting horn, and I realised that Kalle had picked up on it long before we had heard it. I suggested that we wait a bit longer, unclear how this was going to play out. A few minutes later, the local hunt appeared over the hedgerow less than 100 metres away, in the next field to us. As 30 horses jumped over the hedge and galloped past with about the same number of dogs, all barking, Kalle grew increasingly frantic and flew up and down the arena at an alarming rate. It was an incredible sight, but I was terrified in case Kalle jumped the arena fence and joined them. Thankfully she stayed with us, but she continued to gallop up and down for the next 45 minutes.

My workshop was over. There was no way we could work with Kalle now. She was drenched in sweat and far too anxious for clients to lead safely. I couldn't get near her. Throughout, I noticed brief moments when I wanted someone to come along and take over. I wanted someone to fix the "problem" and ease my discomfort of not knowing. I kept bringing myself back to focus on the clients, knowing that they were relying on me to lead. I stayed, grounded in my leadership, trusting that somehow we could recover the situation in some way, trusting that the clients would be OK with the workshop ending this way.

The clients never finished their day as Kalle remained agitated and unsafe to lead. I offered them a free afternoon session another day so that they could complete their learning. Weeks later, they had still not returned, and when I contacted them again, they explained that they had got the learning they needed. The learning had been around how to stay in the discomfort of not knowing what is going to happen next and how to respond to it powerfully as a leader, continuing to take responsibility for our actions without needing everything to be wrapped up perfectly with a pretty bow on top. They learned that leadership is messy, and that we can still lead effectively even when we are uncomfortable and have no idea what to do next. My first workshop had thrown me in at the deep end of uncertainty.

Being uncomfortable

Uncertainty is uncomfortable. We naturally seek comfort and safety, and we therefore avoid uncertainty. Many of my clients talk about being in control as if it were something to strive for. One of the reasons people gravitate towards others like themselves is because they know how those people will think and act. It creates a place of certainty and safety.

We are never in control. Leadership happens out of the comfort zone, in times of uncertainty. Whenever there is a lack of clarity, there is discomfort, a sense of not knowing the destination or how to get there. The challenge is to stay with the discomfort long enough to allow something new to emerge.

When there is uncertainty, we leave the comfort zone and our default patterns of behaviour show up under stress conditions. An eventual breakthrough is the reward when leaders develop the tenacity and a willingness to keep going in service of something greater than the self. When the ego kicks in and we become attached to a particular outcome, the uncertainty is more uncomfortable. When we surrender to what is happening, we can navigate our way forward, trusting that step by step we create the new. It requires a huge amount of flexibility and a trust in our ability to create the future from what is presented.

How can you be more comfortable with uncertainty?

In the current climate of great uncertainty, we need more balance. When people are repeatedly put under pressure, they become stressed. While this is a normal response to the discomfort of uncertainty, we need to develop the skills to stay and lead through the discomfort before reaching a state of overwhelm. Taking time out to recharge ensures that we can be resilient. Many leaders in organisations are exhausted due to the repeated pressure of leading through uncertainty. Recovery is an essential part of leading through uncertainty, and we need to create space for it.

Disconnection and disengagement

With the increasing use of technology, we rarely switch off. Whenever there is discomfort, people reach for their phones as a way of distracting themselves. We seek comfort in the knowledge that there will always be a way of connecting with others through social media, email or by escaping through playing games. Distraction is a form of disconnection. There is a desire to move away when things get uncomfortable. Notice what your patterns are in a team when things are not going well.

Where do you withdraw and what is the impact of that?

Disconnection can show up in lots of ways, for example the moment you get frustrated in a meeting and switch off, however briefly. Or the time someone is talking and you disagree so you roll your eyes and disconnect. You get stuck in your own thoughts and ways of thinking, believing others to be wrong and you to be right. You retreat to listening to self as a form of protection and shut out the needs of others. All of this creates disconnection and prevents collaboration. At times, listening to self is needed for your safety and to make sense of your thoughts. It is important to notice it, recover and reconnect when it feels appropriate.

Disconnection and disengagement are a normal part of the discomfort of uncertainty. We don't need to fight it, either in ourselves or in others. Developing the muscle of reconnection and re-engagement involves paying attention to the disconnection and bringing yourself back. Fear has a huge part to play in the disconnection. Often people withdraw through a desire to maintain their safety or to avoid conflict. By overcoming the voice of fear, it grows easier, with practice, to be true to yourself in thought and action, and the ability to stay becomes second nature.

We need to allow disconnection to happen, for ourselves and for others, and not see it as a broken system, and to trust that it can be balanced with re-engagement. The responsibility lies with each individual to be aware of their patterns of behaviour and to recover and recalibrate more quickly.

How can you support people in your team to disconnect and reconnect without blame or judgement, knowing that the baseline for disconnection is different for everyone?

When people disconnect, it does not mean that trust is necessarily broken, although people often think it is. Continuing to trust, respect and build relationships can help people re-engage and feel supported rather than isolated. Relationships require continual attention and connection is not a one-off event. It requires ongoing nurturing, and this is especially important when people disengage. The tendency is to take it person-ally when you see others disconnect. When you recognise the disconnection as a way of managing the discomfort, you can create acceptance for the ebb and flow of connection and disconnection. When people disconnect, it becomes harder to reconnect because they lose their sense of belonging. If you see disconnection as part of the process, you can show support and stay open, and it is easier for people to re-engage more quickly. Everyone will disconnect and reconnect at different moments, based on where they are triggered and where their comfort zone lies. When there is acceptance that disconnection is part of the process, people feel more comfortable dealing with the discomfort in different ways and that reduces the pressure on everyone.

Holding polarities and paradox

Difference isn't chaos, although it often looks and feels as though it is because we seek the comfort of certainty and alignment. We need to be able to hold polarities in uncertainty as we navigate challenges with different opinions and approaches. This is magnified when we work globally with different cultural beliefs and value systems. Polarities and paradox can lead to disconnection due to the discomfort of perceived conflict. The chaos and conflict that arise from different opinions are part of the process of leading through uncertainty. Therefore it is essential that leaders develop the skills in this area to work in harmony with themselves and with each other. Co-sensing and co-shaping the future is a crucial part of this.

Many people struggle with not knowing, and rewards and recognition have historically been based on knowledge and information. Now the leadership requirements are changing – the discomfort of difference is something that leaders will increasingly experience and therefore need to adapt to.

> *Holding polarities and paradox can be uncomfortable, as the answers are unclear and unknown. Polarities provide an opportunity for dialogue, discussion and collaboration, as long as we accept that it will be uncomfortable and that we need to stay engaged.*

We can increase creativity and innovation and build deeper relationships with other members of the team, once we know how to hold them with curiosity.

Where might you be shutting down polarities out of a desire for comfort and answers?

Polarised views can be destructive, so we need to continually develop the skills of holding them, without resorting to blame, judgement and criticism. When clients work with the horses, they often discover that the horse may have a different opinion and refuse to move when asked. Initially, clients are uncomfortable because their sole aim is to move the horse. Their attachment to the end goal causes them to blame the horse for being stubborn or difficult. In fact, the horse is very willing and engaged but is waiting for clarity before they move forward. The horses show a way of being ok with difference, without losing trust and breaking the relationship. By contrast, when people cannot get the horse to do what they want, they become frustrated and want to control and have their own way. They assume the relationship is broken even though it isn't. Increasing control in uncertainty is counter-productive and the horses invite clients to find a way to provide clarity and direction balanced with flexibility and dialogue.

Creating clarity

With uncertainty comes perceived chaos as things rarely progress in a linear form. The need for clarity may cause people to become controlling and coercive as they want to resolve the discomfort quickly and reach consensus. Yet clarity and control are fundamentally different. The increasing uncertainty of our time requires us to relinquish control and relax into flexibility and adaptability, trusting that we can create clarity as we lead through it.

Uncertainty and clarity can co-exist

Dialogue can occur only when you are clear about your needs, values and beliefs. It is important to let go of being attached to being right because values are not right or wrong. Everyone holds different values and beliefs, and we can hold multiple opinions to be true at any one time.

Often when there is difference, people hide behind a mask. There is a desire to belong to the "we agree" club, yet differences are normal and actively to be encouraged in an increasingly globalised workplace. The very nature of uncertainty means that there is no one right/wrong answer. Instead, there are multiple views of how to move forward.

We can create clarity by expressing the differences without attachment to the need for one answer and without jumping to conclusions or trying to force alignment quickly. Innovation arises from exploration, which requires openness and clarity to create understanding. Understanding is different from agreement and we can create understanding through clarity, without needing to agree.

Where can you create more clarity and understanding?

When uncertainty is uncomfortable and views appear to be polarised, you can explore the values and boundaries of others while being clear about your own values and boundaries of what is acceptable and what is not. When you seek to understand what is important to others, you can co-create solutions that could not be considered previously.

> *The desire for certainty means we often seek to have our own view made clear, without allowing others the space to articulate theirs. Part of the discomfort of uncertainty is the ability to stay through heated discussions and polarised views, letting go of the attachment to being right or wrong.*

This is a fundamental shift from the 1990s' style of management through technical know-how and command and control. When you relinquish attachment and control, it is easier to create clarity.

Staying grounded

Anxiety occurs when we are attached to the past or the future. When we focus on avoiding past experiences or become attached to our own view of the future, we are no longer present. It is challenging to stay grounded in the midst of chaos. It is important not to get caught up in the swell of chaos and become a part of it.

Instead, grounded leaders stay present and find ways to alleviate the discomfort without becoming a headless chicken. Many people who have recognised the need for calm have learned to project it externally while feeling something vastly different internally. In order to be congruent and to prevent burnout, we need to find ways to create calm within, not just externally.

The rise of mindfulness and meditation activities has offered people access to this inner calm. It is central to effective leadership. Paying attention to your physical responses to situations provides an invaluable source of information that you can combine with cognitive reasoning. Tension in the body is information that can guide you to think and act differently. By being flexible in your approach and aware of what you are thinking and feeling, you lead in service of the whole rather than in pursuit of individual goals.

Where can you switch your focus to leading in service of the whole?

We create action in the present moment, and we are more effective when that action comes from a place of grounded leadership rather than from a chaotic response to a crisis. When put under pressure, your adrenaline naturally fires up. That's fine for a short period of time, but it can become exhausting for both you and your team if you continually operate from a place of stress.

Learning to be comfortable with not knowing and uncertainty enables us to stay more grounded and not invoke the fight/flight/freeze stress response. This is pivotal to the future of leadership, to minimise stress and overwhelm in uncertainty.

How grounded are you?

With the fast-paced world we live in, being present is a challenge for many people who live and work at break-neck speed.

Spending time with the horses enables people to connect to the natural environment, a well-documented place of rejuvenation and reconnection to self. Horses invite us to a place of stillness from which creativity can occur. Research shows that in the presence of horses, we align our head, heart and gut. We slow down our breathing and heart rate, become more present and experience a clarity that naturally comes from this calm, grounded place. Many leaders have gained clarity over their most pressing problems by finding this inner state of calm in the midst of great uncertainty. They may not find all the answers, but the next step becomes clear and the grounded sense of calm gives them confidence in moving forward into the unknown.

Grounded leaders look after themselves, find moments to disconnect from technology and other people, and find space to recharge. Slowing down enables greater acceptance of the uncertainty and a recognition that it may not be fixable but instead is something to be navigated.

How can you support yourself better through uncertainty?

Effective leaders flex their approach and recalibrate moment by moment. This enables them to stay in the discomfort of uncertainty without needing to create a short-term fix. Breakthroughs always follow uncertainty and chaos. The challenge is to stay grounded in the discomfort long enough to create the transformation.

MASTERING UNCERTAINTY

- Stay with the discomfort of uncertainty and avoid distraction techniques that take you off track.

- Take time out to recharge to minimise stress and overwhelm.

- Allow disconnection and disengagement as part of the process of dealing with uncertainty.

- Stay open and trust that people will reconnect and re-engage when they feel comfortable enough to do so.

- Use polarities as an opportunity for dialogue, discussion and collaboration.

- Seek to understand differences and provide clarity without jumping to conclusions.

- Have compassion for everyone in uncertainty and recognise that the discomfort is tiring over time.

- Continually recalibrate your approach to ease the discomfort for you as well as for your team.

Before you move on to the next chapter, spend 10 minutes reflecting on how you flip between disconnection and connection and how you can stay in the discomfort of uncertainty.

 Download the *Leading Through Uncertainty* workbook from www.judejennison.com/uncertainty and record your reflections.

PROVOKING PERSONAL INSIGHT

How can you be more comfortable with uncertainty?

Where do you withdraw and what is the impact of that?

*How can you support people in your team to disconnect and recon-
nect without blame or judgement, knowing that the baseline for
disconnection is different for everyone?*

*Where might you be shutting down polarities out of a desire for
comfort and answers?*

Where can you create more clarity and understanding?

Where can you switch your focus to leading in service of the whole?

How grounded are you?

How can you support yourself better through uncertainty?

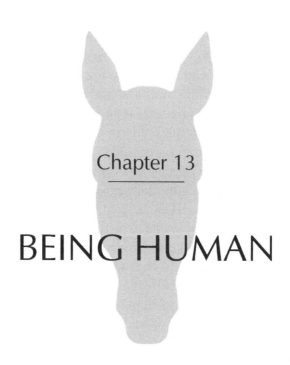

Chapter 13

BEING HUMAN

*"Leadership is about finding ease and flow amidst
the chaos and struggle."*

Rachel held back. Everyone knew that she had her own horses.
She had been deemed "the expert" and the expectations were
high. As Rachel watched her peers lead a horse one by one, her
anxiety rose. She knew that this was different. Leading a horse
was something she did every day, but she had never done it with
the Leaders by Nature horses. Her horsemanship skills were not
going to be enough here. This required her leadership skills.

Rachel realised that my horses would not move just because
they were told to. They don't respond to command and control,
and they won't respond to horsemanship techniques. They have

an opinion and are not afraid to use it. If they don't want to move, they won't.

As Rachel took the lead rope, she was anxious. She felt under pressure to perform in the spotlight, and she doubted her capabilities as a leader in that moment, as people often do when things are uncertain. She held the lead rope tightly beneath Kalle's chin. She gave a sharp tug to ask Kalle to go with her, and Kalle headbutted her. Rachel stopped and Kalle headbutted her again. Rachel was used to telling her horses what to do and expecting them to follow. Kalle doesn't work like that. She won't respond to control and demands. She wants to be inspired, engaged and led, just like people in the workplace. Kalle also likes to fully express her opinion. She couldn't do that with the lead rope being so short and tight. She was resisting being micro-managed.

I asked Rachel to lengthen the lead rope so that Kalle could move her head. Rachel let go of control and found herself unsure how to lead. I'd removed her usual way of leading a horse, and she needed to find a new approach. Rachel stood still, trying to work it out. The more she analysed what was going on, the more disconnected she became from Kalle, and the more Kalle refused to move. Rachel had put herself under pressure to meet the expectations of both herself and her peers, who thought she would make it look easy. The longer she stood there, the more pressure she put herself under. The rest of her team looked on, amazed. Self-imposed performance anxiety is limiting and derailing.

I asked Rachel what she thought Kalle needed from her as a leader.

"Clarity, direction and connection," Rachel replied.

"Which of those is missing?" I asked.

"All of them!" Rachel laughed. She realised that she needed to relax into her leadership. She took a couple of breaths, trusted herself and invited Kalle to walk with her. They walked round effortlessly. Rachel walked with confidence and ease. Once she had let go of control, she could step into her leadership. Kalle was engaged at last.

Authentic leadership

Clients often judge a task as difficult before they start. I often say to them, "Have it be easy." We put ourselves under immense pressure for lots of reasons – when we are deemed to be "the expert", when others have high expectations of us, when we are in the spotlight, being watched, when we have challenging deadlines or targets to meet, when we fear failure, and many more. Many clients feel the pressure of being observed, and they over-analyse how to lead. Leadership is largely something we feel. We know when we are in flow, and we know when it feels awkward and clunky. When clients work with the horses, they experience both. I liken it to riding a bike – you know when you are balanced and you know when you are wobbling! Leadership requires us to repeatedly find the balance and flow.

Rachel had put herself under so much pressure that she became focused on herself and her colleagues watching her. While she was in her head trying to work out how to move a horse, the connection with Kalle was lost, and she failed to lead.

Where are you focused on your own performance and results and have lost connection with others?

Whenever you lack trust in yourself, there is a tendency to hide behind a mask. Horses refuse to engage with the masks. They connect with the real person beneath the masks and barriers. If your external behaviour does not match your internal behaviour, it is incongruent, and the horses refuse to engage. They won't work with mixed messages. If you want to lead a horse, you have to be real, honest, open and vulnerable. People want the real you, too.

To be authentic requires us to trust ourselves first, to trust that we are safe when we are vulnerable, that we can lead effectively through the unknown. Once Rachel let go of needing to be perfect, she was able to lead with ease.

Case study – John*

John was known for being brutal with his team. He chose to work with Kalle, who will not move without connection and relationship. To everyone's surprise, he stroked her on the neck and invited her to come with him. As he walked forward, he was clear where he was going, he was connected to Kalle, and she went with him willingly. He was kind and gentle and offered reassurance all the way round. When he came back to where the team were standing, he thanked her and stroked her again. His team stood with their mouths open.

When I asked John about the experience, he said he thought it was easier to be kind to a horse than to a person. He explained that if he was gentle at work, he didn't think he'd be respected. One member of his team said he respected John more because now he knew that John was human. There was a moment when everyone in the team paused for breath. John's fear of being vulnerable had prevented him from being compassionate at work, even though it was a trait he was able to demonstrate easily.

Once he realised that compassion and gratitude were strengths and appreciated by his team, John was more caring towards them at work. John's natural style was to care about his team, but he was hiding behind the mask of "needing to be respected". It prevented him from building relationships with them and showing that he cared. He had judged it as a weakness and was incongruent in his behaviour. Once John was honest about how he really felt, he and his team were more relaxed together and their relationships improved.

* Name changed to protect confidentiality

Leaders who pay attention to their inner dialogue as well as the outer dialogue attune themselves to their gut instinct and emotions, along with the logical information in the brain. When leaders operate out of their comfort zone, there is a tendency to hold back or push through the discomfort, both of which lack authenticity. By bringing more of yourself to a situation and being honest about how it feels for you, you can engage authentically with others and work together with honesty and integrity. We need to foster an environment in which people feel safe to bring more of themselves into their work and understand the benefits of doing so.

Letting go

When teams walk through my gate, their bodies are often tense and conversation is either loud, anxious and boisterous or subdued, reflective and restrained. Either approach is born from the stress of being out of the comfort zone. There is regularly a wave of energy based on ego, positioning, a need to "get it right" and save face. It is often matched only by a wave of exhaustion from overwork.

Uncertainty is uncomfortable. People desire to hang on to what is known. It's uncomfortable standing in a field about to get honest feedback on your leadership skills... from a horse! Some are sceptical and dismissive, greeting me with "I don't see the point of this". Others are quiet and reflective, anxious that they may be "found out" as not being a good leader. Some are excited about a new experience. Others want to get going quickly before the anxiety takes over.

These are all natural states of responding to not knowing. Each person shows up with their default approach to uncertainty, without realising it. Their default habits and behaviours are unconscious until they work with the horses. Everyone has to let go of who they want to be seen as and step into their authentic leadership.

What is your default approach to uncertainty?

Most education systems are founded on a right or wrong approach. You are rewarded for getting the right answer and reprimanded for doing the wrong thing. This black/white, right/wrong approach is useful for developing a moral compass and cognitive processing like basic maths, but the skills we require to lead through uncertainty require a different style of leadership. A right or wrong approach comes with blame, judgement and criticism. They are not part of leadership! It assumes that there is only one way of doing things. We struggle to define what leadership is because it is something that we largely feel. You know when you are in flow and you know when you are not.

Leading through uncertainty requires huge flexibility and adaptability. There is no right or wrong because the answers are unknown, and therefore the approach is untried and untested.

Mr Blue creates a distraction

When we let go of needing to be right, we can foster an environment that encourages people to take the next step not knowing where it will take them. New possibilities and opportunities can emerge when we act with curiosity.

Tension comes from attachment, a desire to make things black and white, and for our opinion to be right. It is human to want to do a good job, and we want to encourage great work, but we can do it without creating the stress. In writing this book, I was up against a deadline. With only a week to go, I still had two chapters to finish. I felt my anxiety rise as meeting the deadline became in doubt. I didn't want to fail. I was using up critical energy worrying about the deadline. Once I let go of needing to meet the deadline, I allowed myself to focus on the writing. I met the deadline, but more importantly I let go of all the stress around meeting it. I set myself free.

With stretch targets and high workloads, it is unrealistic to be able to achieve everything on our to-do list. We need to relinquish the control we want to have over work and find a new way of being in relationship with it.

What outcome are you attached to and where is that causing tension?

It is important to let go. When we let go, we trust in our leadership. We trust that whatever happens, we can deal with it. By letting go of control, we step into the discomfort of not knowing and difference.

Letting go does not mean that you absolve yourself of all responsibility. You still hold the desire and the intention, without the attachment to the minute details. When you relinquish the stress and tension of attachment, your leadership can flow more easily.

Uncertainty can be expansive. It generates new ways of doing things which may not match your vision of the ideal. The paradigm shift from command and control to collective leadership requires you as a leader to relinquish control, to provide a steer, set the direction and let go so that the collective team can create fluidly within a framework. If people do not feel supported or empowered in uncertainty, they feel unsafe. The difference between support and control is monumental, and leaders often confuse the two. Uncertainty is a natural part of the human condition, and we avoid it wherever we can. It is easy to be reactive and try to lock down the uncertainty into that which is certain. We need to develop the skills to be with uncertainty without resorting to stress, overwhelm, fear and polarisation.

Control and power are illusions. When we relinquish control and power over situations or people, we can step into the skills needed to create harmony in relationships. Once we realise that the uncertainty is challenging for everyone, we can provide support to each other and navigate it together as a collective.

Ease and flow

People flourish when you remove the fear of failure. When you let go, you allow room for failure and error, and you develop the skills of flexibility, adaptability and agility. When you relax and trust, you can become more courageous and entrepreneurial. We all have days when we feel on fire. Everything is effortless and easy, and nothing can stop us. We also have times when our leadership feels challenging and clumsy. Conversations feel difficult, meetings don't go according to plan, deadlines are missed, people don't do what we want them to do. Frustration builds. This is part of being human. We have emotions, and we can use them to inform and guide us.

Our best leadership is when we return to the place of ease and flow, without the tension of fear, stress and attachment. Life is full of ups and downs. The drive for positive psychology and happiness increases the unnecessary pressure we put upon ourselves when things are not going according to plan. We fight the challenges and are not satisfied until everything is in flow again.

Margaret Wheatley encourages us to accept the ups and the downs of life in her book *Perseverance*: "It can take many years of being battered by events and people to discover clarity the other side of the struggle. This clarity is not about how to win, but about how to be, how to withstand life's challenges, how to stay in the river.

"Once we've experienced life in all its dimensions – good, bad, hard, easy – life doesn't seem so challenging. Every situation is what it is, sometimes lovely, sometimes difficult. Every situation is workable".[10]

We can make leadership a struggle or we can allow it to be easy. Notice the difference. We "make" it a struggle or we "allow" it to be easy. The struggle requires a pushing, coercive energy – the desire for a specific end goal where there is no room for flexing. Allowing creates opportunities, enables new ways, new ideas, new possibilities. It allows for listening and dialogue, co-sensing and co-shaping, and trusts that there will be a breakthrough if you stay in the discomfort of uncertainty.

Where can you allow your leadership to flow more effortlessly?

Struggle creates tension, allowing just flows, trusting that we can lead and respond to anything that shows up. The energy used to struggle creates tension and stress. When you find your flow, you release the energy of stress and tension, and everything becomes easier. This is an embodied way of leading, where you sense into the tension in your body and allow it to be released by letting go and trusting.

Compassion

Everyone who chooses to lead will experience the glory of success and results, as well as the crushing defeat of failure. We are human after all. With the highs, come the lows. To avoid the lows denies us the full human experience. Organisations with a culture of fear of failure inhibit innovation and creativity and create stress and pressure.

---

[10] M. Wheatley, Perseverance, Berrett-Koehler Publishers (2010).

We sometimes forget to be human. In the pursuit of doing great work, achieving goals and meeting deadlines and targets, we exert pressure on ourselves and others to avoid failure at all cost. While pressure can enhance our performance for a short period of time, it is not sustainable over longer periods. The cost of excessive pressure is poor physical, emotional and mental health.

Clients connect when they slow down

We need more compassion in business – compassion for those who are struggling as well as compassion for ourselves. We need to shift from trying to be machines in a world of technology to using technology to allow ourselves to be human. When we accept our humanity, we can be kinder to ourselves and to others.

We live and work in a time of significant pressure. The workload volume is immense, and the pressures outside of work continue to grow in parallel. The expectations we place upon ourselves for what we can achieve are often unrealistic. We blame others for that pressure – it's your boss's fault, the shareholders' expectations or the person in your team who is slowing you down by not doing what you want them to do. There is a tension between what is humanly possible and what we think we can achieve in the timescales available.

In this fast-paced techno world, we sometimes attempt to be superhuman. We forget to be kind, compassionate and considerate towards ourselves. We focus on the results we want to achieve and sometimes on the relationships we want to create or maintain with others. In the process, self-care is overlooked and expectations are unrealistic.

Where do you fit in your daily life?

Often people want to be given permission to be compassionate. They consider it a weakness until they realise how essential it is for themselves as well as for their team. Considerate leaders include and embrace everything. They hold compassion for people experiencing challenges. That includes having compassion for yourself as well.

How senior leaders behave sets the tone for the organisation. Having compassion for yourself and others shows that there is space for humanity, knowing that you will never have 100% full capacity from every single person on every single day.

Having compassion means choosing to act with self-care and choosing to minimise stress and overwhelm. It may mean saying no to unrealistic targets and deadlines, or taking time out to recover and recharge after an especially busy or stressful period at work.

In an interview in January 2018, Sue Grindrod, CEO of the Albert Dock in Liverpool, explained: "I make sure that I take time out for me. It's important to be kind to yourself, especially when you are under pressure, and to be realistic about what you can actually achieve. If you try to cram everything in, you set yourself up for overwhelm".[11]

How do you hold yourself with compassion when you are struggling, too?

Who in your team is suffering and needs your compassion?

Case study – Nigel*

"Move over there," demanded Nigel, pointing to a place on the ground. Kalle stood still, eyes half closed, not moving. As Nigel grew increasingly exasperated by a horse who appeared unwilling and uncooperative, he turned to me and said vehemently, "This horse is stubborn and won't do it."

I calmly asked Nigel what he did with people in his team who did not do what he asked them to do. He said he got rid of them. His desire for results was so great that he had no empathy for anyone in his team.

I explained that Kalle wanted kindness, and he was astonished. He had never considered that there might be a different way, and he had no idea how to find it. He had a high turnover in his organisation and could not understand why. As soon as it was pointed out to him, Nigel realised that he had been letting good people leave his business, and he wanted to change that. Throughout the day, Nigel learned to soften his approach and give the horse an opinion. As he did so, he found the horse more engaged and more willing to work with him. Some months later, Nigel reported that he was taking time to connect with everyone in his organisation and that relationships and teamwork had improved.

* Name changed to protect confidentiality

---

[11] Leaders by Nature podcast (2018). Available from: www.judejennison.com/podcast/podcast-8-sue-grindrod-ceo-albert-dock-liverpool [accessed 20 January 2018].

Compassion for self and others is imperative in challenging times, yet we often overlook it. Continuing to drive ourselves as machines leads to burnout. It's the responsibility of every leader to look out for their team and consider their needs.

It's time to revert to the core of our humanity, to remember that we are human beings having a human experience. Most of us work in fast-paced changing businesses that require us to be superhuman. We are not machines. It's up to each and every leader to to decide on what is humanly possible and to recognise that the benchmark of that is different for everyone.

MASTERING UNCERTAINTY

- Be open, honest and transparent and drop the masks.

- Let go of control and attachment and be curious about possibilities.

- Take responsibility for your actions.

- Find your ease and flow and keep returning to it.

- Switch from "struggling" to "allowing".

- Be kind, compassionate and considerate.

- Say no to unrealistic targets.

- Have compassion for those who are suffering.

- Ease pressure and stress for yourself and others.

Before you move on to the next chapter, spend 10 minutes reflecting on how you can be more human.

 Download the *Leading Through Uncertainty* workbook from www.judejennison.com/uncertainty and record your reflections.

PROVOKING PERSONAL INSIGHT

Where are you focused on your own performance and results and have lost connection with others?

What is your default approach to uncertainty?

What outcome are you attached to and where is that causing tension?

Where can you allow your leadership to flow more effortlessly?

Where do you fit in your daily life?

How do you hold yourself in compassion when you are struggling, too?

Who in your team is suffering and needs your compassion?

Chapter 14

LEADING FROM THE HEART AND SOUL

"Leading with passion and purpose
brings people alive."

When Kalle arrived in December 2011, I sensibly put her in a full livery yard so that someone else could look after her, and I could learn from them. With my lack of horse knowledge, I needed all the support I could get, and I thought this would ease the pressure for me. It didn't. The livery yard handled their horses very differently, using coercion and control. I learned a lot about how I did not want to be in relationship with Kalle. To be clear, these were kind people who loved their horses, but in the same way that people in business use force and control to get people to do things, they expected their horses to follow the rules, too.

I had different ideas and different values. I wanted to lead Kalle in a way that enabled her to keep her majestic spirit and to live and work with free will. I want the same for people in my team, too. The relationship I wanted to have with Kalle was one of partnership, respect, trust, love and connection. I refused to resort to force or dominance, but I was unskilled in knowing another way. That's what uncertainty often brings – a need for trial and error. Fail, recover and begin again.

In the first few days, Kalle ran rings round me, sometimes literally. She was often on her toes, spinning round in front of me, snorting in fear. She spooked at everything. I mirrored her fear, terrified she might trample me or knock me over. I had no idea how to look after a horse, and I was finding my way, working it out as I went along. I ignored the books and the contradictory horsemanship advice and followed my intuition. I drew on every ounce of my corporate leadership experience to understand Kalle's needs and develop a relationship. I knew that every time Kalle took the lead, it was because she didn't have confidence in my leadership, so I had to keep stepping up. I listened and paid attention to her feedback and tried a different approach.

The yard staff became increasingly irritated with me for not following their coercive instructions. They said she was naughty and needed to be slapped. I saw her fear and wanted to help her find her confidence instead. I knew that my leadership and my own confidence in uncertainty would be the breakthrough that we both needed. The control they used with their horses, they also tried to use with their clients like me. While other clients did as they were told and slapped their horses, I refused to. My stress levels began to rise. I so badly wanted to fit in, but I was clearly very different, not least because I didn't ride. I wanted to learn from their experience, but I knew that when I followed my instincts and really listened to Kalle, we understood what our way was. We were co-sensing and co-shaping our future.

True relationship, true partnership, true co-creation. I was unskilled in knowing how to create that with a horse in those early days. Every night I went home in tears and told my husband I couldn't do it any more. He sat and listened without judgement. When I asked whether I should give it up or continue, he always responded that he knew I would find my way and make my own decisions.

I stayed. I stayed when I was face down in mud with concussion. I stayed when Kalle electrocuted us both and reared up, retriggering my trauma around horses. I stayed when we looked each other in the eye in a moment of pure connection as we collapsed on our knees when the farrier beat her for not standing still. I stayed even though I sobbed uncontrollably for two hours afterwards. I stayed through one drama after another (many documented in my previous book, *Leadership Beyond Measure*) because sometimes leading from the heart and soul requires it and because I was leading in service of my clients who were gaining breakthroughs from working with us. Every morning, I got up and tried again. Over the first six months, I was in and out of overwhelm. I had no idea how to look after a horse and no idea how to run a business either, and here I was trying to learn both in parallel.

I became exhausted and overwhelmed by the responsibility. I had gone beyond the realm of uncertainty to unskilled and unsafe. Something had to change. I sought help from Kalle's previous owner and asked her to take Kalle back temporarily. She provided support for the next six weeks while I rebuilt my confidence and found a new place for Kalle to live, a place where we could both relax and find our way together without being told what to do and without needing to use force of any kind. I created a framework of support so that I could continue.

I'm still here, leading and learning. While I have more skill, my own land and the most incredibly relaxed and happy herd, the uncertainty continues. On a daily basis, uncertainty rears its head, and I find a way to move forward.

*Jude leading four of her herd (left to right, Kalle,
Tiffin, Jude, Mr Blue, Gio)*

Embodying uncertainty

Uncertainty requires us to step into the unknown. We may think we know where we are going, but we don't always know how to get there. Along the way, things pop up that we cannot foresee and that we cannot fathom. Somehow, we recover and carry on, including those new experiences and the associated learning in our path. I recently called out a vet to treat a horse while working with a client team. Imagine my horror as I stood talking to clients and saw out of the corner of my eye that blood was pouring out of my horse's foot and running down the yard. Despite it looking like a scene from a horror movie, I somehow stayed focused on giving the clients an outstanding learning experience, trusting the vet and trusting my yard manager who was holding the horse at the time. The horse's foot thankfully recovered, and the clients had a great day.

There is no manual or how-to guide to deal with the unknown. We lead our way through it, sometimes with ease, sometimes with discomfort.

The path of uncertainty is an emotionally challenging one. I hope this book has given a better understanding of why that is and what that means for you as a leader, as well as how you can support your team and organisation. We cannot pretend that the emotions don't exist.

> *We experience fear and polarisation, stress and overwhelm, in varying degrees, when we lead through uncertainty. We are all resilient to a point, and resilience differs for everyone. We cannot continue to put ourselves under inordinate pressure without realising that it has a long-term impact on individuals, organisations and society. We are humans having a human experience, not computers processing information.*

Technology can support us, hinder us or ruin us. I may work outdoors in a field with horses, but my business would not exist without technology, and my daily life depends on it, too. I hope we learn to use it wisely instead of allowing it to dominate us. It's down to each and every one of us to make powerful choices moment by moment, on both a micro and a macro level.

This book has been challenging to write because it describes *embodied leadership* and it invites you to find *your* new way, which is always going to be different from mine. We can't just plan ahead and expect everything to fall into place and people to do what we want, when we want, how we want. We are not machines. We can't turn emotional responses like fear and stress on and off just by knowing about them. We have to process them, work with them and learn to lessen the grip they have on us, knowing that they will always be a part of leading through uncertainty. That is a work in process – a lifetime of learning and a continuous cycle of increasing self-awareness.

We live in extraordinary times. We have the ability to develop ourselves in unimaginable ways, to evolve the human species through conscious leadership, being mindful of what we do and the impact we have in each and every moment. The skills needed to influence others and create human connection are not easy to develop. We need to embody them and find ways to develop ourselves in a safe environment, with continuous feedback and space for reflection, based on scientific evidence.

It is a privilege for me to witness clients experience this when working with my herd of five horses, who give so freely to enable transformational learning. They invite us to change our world view, to amend our habits and behaviours, to influence the future and create work that is life-enhancing, in a world that we want to leave behind for future generations. That's a big ask from a development experience, yet it's what I offer to my clients.

It's six years since Kalle came into my life. In those six years, I have taken on six horses, helped them recover from previous ailments (physical and emotional) and rehabilitated one of them to go to a new home as he was not safe to work with clients and had recovered sufficiently to be ridden again. I've experienced highs and lows and learned so much. In addition to all the learning with the horses, I set up a business with a business partner and closed it down again when it was no longer working. Sometimes you need the courage to do what feels right. I've set out on my own again, building a solid team around me, safe in the knowledge and wisdom that I know what I am doing and have the ability to lead confidently and securely through uncertainty. Except when I don't. I have my limits, too. I do know that in the brief moments when I falter, I'm building the resilience to come back stronger.

I stay when it is uncomfortable. I always give my best and reflect on the learning, enabling me to continually grow as a leader. That's all you can ask of anyone.

Uncertainty is uncomfortable. It is an opportunity to learn as a leader, to develop new skills, to find new ways of working and to achieve extraordinary things. It can derail us and cause confusion. Whenever we are not in flow, we have the choice to recover to that state, to dig deeper in our leadership, to find new ways of doing things, to fail, recover and try again.

How do you continually modify your behaviour to meet an ever-changing, fast-paced environment?

Leading through uncertainty requires a new mindset. Although emotional and social intelligence increasingly have been recognised as essential components of leadership, they have largely been engaged from the intellect. We need to shift from the analysis of emotions to empathic understanding and emotional engagement.

A new way of leading from the heart and soul is called for as we embrace the next evolution of leadership, with courage and compassion in abundance. Leaders who have a sense of purpose and passion for their work feel alive and are engaging and inspiring to others. They feel compelled to go above and beyond what is expected of them, recognising the emotional fallout of uncertainty, finding new ways of leading from the heart and soul.

Final thoughts

As I stand in the field after a workshop with clients, the horses graze calmly beside me. There is incredible peace around me and within me. Each one of them has taught me so much and will continue to do so. They give freely and willingly, sometimes being gentle with me when I am vulnerable and afraid, sometimes headbutting me into next week when I am dithering and uncertain. That doesn't happen too often!

Kalle in particular expects me to lead from the front. If I don't lead my business and the herd from the front, nobody else will. It's my role and one I step up to with passion, joy and enthusiasm. Most of the time. Sometimes, it feels lonely at the top. I know many CEOs experience that, too. I have plenty of mentors who offer advice and guidance, but ultimately it's my responsibility to lead my business, the herd and my clients. They all expect it of me.

The horses are soft yet powerful. They know their purpose is intertwined with mine – to lead others to find their inner peace so that we all have the skills to live and work in harmony with others. I watch and learn. I notice when they set boundaries and articulate their needs with clarity. I watch Kalle stand solidly in self-assured presence – blending power and gentleness, clarity with compassion. She has a massive range of leadership skills and is an incredible role model of a female leader who loses none of her femininity while standing strongly with a powerful presence.

People often tell me how happy the horses are. My horses move a lot, play a lot and seem utterly content with their life. I want to lead a team who have a zest for life, joy for their work and a desire to make a difference. The horses certainly do all of that. Every horse who has arrived has come with emotional or physical challenges. Over time, I see them relax into the herd, start to bring more and more of their personality and individuality. They become more challenging to lead once they realise they have full expression of their opinion. I'm willing to be challenged, willing to step up as a leader, knowing that they benefit greatly from having full expression of themselves, as people do, too.

Uncertainty requires the flexibility and willingness to keep trying, keep learning, keep making a difference. It matters. Your leadership matters. We live in extraordinary times where everything seems in flux. One of my clients, a CEO of a large corporation, once said, "I have learned to lead from my spirit, and I can't tell you how powerful that is." There was a brief moment when her executive team stood spellbound. It was as if the world had stopped, and everyone held their breath. Then it began again, changed for ever. This is true leadership, from the heart and soul. This is what I wish for everyone to experience, and this is what I wish for the world. I know we can do great things when we lead from our heart and soul, with courage and compassion, with a desire to leave a legacy that matters in the world. I know that matters to you, to me and to everyone.

In the heart of Warwickshire, in the middle of the English countryside, there is a field. A place of uncertainty. A place where you step through the gate into the unknown, unsure whether your leadership stacks up the way you thought it did. There you discover that despite the uncertainty, you are safe, you are held and you are powerful. The horses and I will meet you there. Join us. The world needs you.

With love,
Jude

MEET THE EQUINE TEAM

Every business needs a high-performing team, and I'm grateful to have handpicked mine. All of my horses are rescue horses. They have been retired from riding careers for various reasons. None of them can now be ridden, so they come to me to do a new job.

I choose horses who are safe to work with novices because the majority of clients have no experience around horses, and many people are anxious on arrival. Every horse that has come to me has a new sense of purpose and when I take them, I commit to providing a home for life. That's a big responsibility, especially when the youngest is only seven. I'm aware that I could be looking after him in my 70s.

Each of my horses has started working with clients within days of arrival. They are curious about the work and interested. Often when we work with one or two horses in the arena, the others will stand at the fence line, watching. The newer ones learn by observing the experienced ones, much as a human team would, too. They all bring different skills and respond in different ways, with vastly different personalities, which often surprises people.

I keep them as a natural herd as much as possible, and they live out in the fields 24/7, all year round. People often comment on how happy the horses seem and how much they play. I think if we provide an environment where people or horses can thrive, they are happy and want to do their best work. That's certainly true of my team. I'm often asked whether I train the horses to do their work. I don't train them, but I encourage them to be true to the core behaviours of their equine species and to express their opinion fully.

As I do not ride the horses, they soon learn that they have a lot of opinion. They don't have to do anything they don't want to do, so they become more challenging to lead because they respond based on my leadership rather than what is expected. Once you work on the ground and invite the horse to have full expression of their opinion, their behaviour begins to change. When they first arrive, they typically do what I ask of them. Over time, they realise they have more opinion than they've ever had before. My relationship with each horse changes continually as they learn that there are still boundaries, but that those boundaries are now different. I invite rather than ask, influence rather than demand. The horses have huge respect for me because I have created it with them by being clear about my boundaries and being equally respectful towards them.

Allow me to introduce you to the current Leaders by Nature team.

Kalle

 Kalle is a black 16.2 hands Trakehner mare, born in April 2000. Trakehners are a German breed and a mix of Arab and thoroughbred breeding. They are highly sensitive, and often riders describe them as tricky. In fact, I find them to be very straightforward and extremely suitable for my work. They want to work in partnership, and they don't like to be told what to do. It makes them ideal for this work because they need you to balance absolute clarity and direction with a strong relationship,

and to invite them to work with you, not for you. If you listen to them and pay attention to their needs, they are very willing.

Kalle was my first horse and started this work in January 2012. She is highly intuitive and she knows which buttons to press to give you great learning. She has a massive range and can bring whatever is needed to give clients the best learning. She will headbutt you into next week if she thinks you are not listening to her or not giving her enough respect. By contrast, she will treat you like a foal if you are terrified. She knows when to challenge and when to back off and be gentle. She can switch from one end of her leadership range to the other in an instant.

When she first arrived, she was often on her toes, snorting in fear at everything that was new. Her power was obvious and explicit, yet clients were willing to work with her, wanting to challenge themselves and learn. Now she has a self-assured presence that people often find intimidating. Many clients avoid her at the beginning of the day, thinking she will be challenging. In fact, she is extremely gentle and kind, and as long as you blend clarity, direction and relationship in equal measure, she follows you anywhere willingly. Learning from her is guaranteed.

While Kalle is hugely committed to helping clients learn, she accepts nothing less than my very best leadership. She is the leader of the herd, so when she moves, everyone else follows. She therefore requires a confident, clear leader before she will relinquish her lead. In moments of uncertainty, she demands that I lead from the front, with confidence, clarity and purpose. She'll have nothing to do with me unless I am on top form. She reminds me that even when I am uncertain, I have a choice to be a powerful leader or not.

It is a privilege to work and learn with her.

Opus

Opus joined me in July 2012, aged 24. He is a 16.1 hands dark brown thoroughbred. He is a descendant of a horse called Northern Dancer, the highest-earning racehorse of all time. Opus was born in Australia in 1988 and lived in New Zealand, Bahrain and then the UK, so he is well travelled and the most experienced of the herd in terms of riding. He has competed in just about everything with his owner, Laura. He makes it clear that he is wise, and he willingly shares his experience.

Opus retired from an extensive riding career and started his new work with clients almost immediately. I call him the Managing Director because nothing happens on the yard without his approval. Clients laugh at this, but at the end of a day in his presence, they realise how true this is. Opus retired from Leadership with Horses work in 2014 as he was getting tired. While he is the only horse not owned by me, I continue to care for him in his full retirement. It feels important to be with him as he ends his days.

When Opus was in work, he was challenging with CEOs, MDs, executive teams and senior leaders because he expected them to lead without dominance. With graduates, he was gentle and easy, so they went away with more confidence. He is the master of fine-tuning in leadership and seemed to know when to raise the bar and be challenging and when to be more gentle.

When I first took Opus on, he literally ran rings round me. Anyone who leads him will experience him looking them up and down, deciding they know nothing and taking charge. He has taught both me and my clients how to balance power with gentleness. Whereas Kalle requires a softer energy, Opus needs a strong, masculine energy in order for him to pay attention. However, if you raise your energy too much, you can easily enter a power struggle with him. There is a subtle difference between "power with" and "power over" and Opus demands that you find that knife-edge of assertiveness in order for him to come with you.

Opus often appears aloof at first as he doesn't connect with people by wanting lots of strokes and hugs. He can be the one at the far end of the field who seems to be disconnected, but he misses nothing. He often has the run of the yard and is the welcoming party to clients. The commitment that he continues to have to me, the herd, clients and leadership is quite incredible. Just like Kalle, Opus demands that I am a powerful leader in uncertainty.

Tiffin

Tiffin was the third horse to join me, in June 2014, at the age of 13. He is a dark bay 16.3 hands Irish thoroughbred, born in Ireland in April 2001. He raced in Ireland and was brought to England to hunt. He was sold every year for four  consecutive years. The last place he lived was a riding school where he sometimes did great work and sometimes exploded and bucked everyone off.

Having been sold repeatedly, and his home never being quite right for him, I was Tiffin's last chance at life – a responsibility I take very seriously. When he had his meltdown (described in Chapter 6), I wondered whether he would be better with a more experienced horse owner, but I persevered as I wanted him to find security in his home. I'm glad I did as he has turned a major corner in his work and is gaining in confidence and trust.

When Tiffin arrived, he looked older than his years. His face was misshapen, and I thought he had possibly taken a tumble during his racing or hunting days to cause this. Over time, as he has relaxed into his home, his face has become gentler, he looks younger, and I realise that his misshapen look was the tension of stress and anxiety.

Tiffin had a difficult start in life and connects deeply with others who have physical or emotional challenges. He will often connect with the person who is emotionally struggling, or he will touch injured parts of the body with his nose. He struggles to work with dominant men, as I believe they remind him of his past. He supports Kalle in leading the herd and keeps the young boys in check. He has become more playful as he relaxes and is often the one to instigate a boxing match with the young boys, inviting them to rise up on their hind legs and play with him.

Tiffin works better on a one-to-one basis as he often finds the energy and anxiety of a team too overwhelming. Tiffin is deep and highly sensitive. He has difficulty trusting people, but if you trust him absolutely, he will join you in that place.

Mr Blue

Mr Blue arrived in October 2015, aged only five years. He is a 16.2 grey Trakehner gelding. He had arthritis by the age of five, which meant he was severely lame when he came to me. He was still a very young horse who had no idea where his feet were and often stumbled over them and made us laugh. Three years later, while he will never be ridden, he moves more smoothly and his feet, back and knees are much stronger.

Mr Blue loves people and is highly interactive. He is the class clown and likes to goof around. He pushes the boundaries and took the longest to integrate into the herd because he didn't pay attention to herd behaviour. He invades personal space repeatedly, and the other horses have to be very clear with him. He does it gently, out of a desire for a close connection, but needs to be put in his place regularly.

He does the same with people and likes to pick up their feet with his teeth. If you let him, he pushes the boundaries further, and he has been known to steal hats and gloves from clients. Mr Blue provides a lot of the humour and fun on workshop days. He loves toys and is easily distracted, so he causes teams to get derailed on a regular basis unless they are extremely focused and clear and work as a cohesive unit.

Mr Blue reminds us not to take life so seriously and to make leadership fun. He also shows how to balance playfulness without losing respect or focus. Often clients who get easily distracted or love to play have a hard time with him because he takes advantage of them. He leads people to become derailed by messing about and causing a distraction. Mr Blue teaches clients the balance of when to have fun and when to be focused to get the job done.

Gio

Gio joined the Leaders by Nature team in June 2017 at the age of seven. He is Mr Blue's half-brother, although they look very different. He is a 17.2 hands black Trakehner gelding who has never been ridden due to ongoing lameness. He has the sweetest personality, and this was his first job.

Although Gio is the largest of the herd by far, he is the gentlest, and he connects on a deep level. He likes to nuzzle your ear and breathe into your nose. He is the first to look up when you go into the field and often the first horse to come over. He is interested in all clients and loves the work. He has learned quickly what is expected of him and is gentle in his teaching to clients. He creates a heart-to-heart connection and is often the one that clients want to take home at the end of the day. He trusts people willingly and readily.

When Gio arrived in June 2017, he was severely lame in all four legs, and his back, neck and knees were all out of place. As a result of being lame since birth and not being ridden, he has grown rapidly without knowing how to use his body. He now has a regular back treatment with a specialist and has gained more strength and confidence in his body since his arrival. While he will never be ridden, he is already moving more fluidly and learning how to move his body. My hope is that he will continue to move more easily and smoothly within the next 18 months as we continue to ease his lameness.

Within six months of arrival, Gio began boxing with Mr Blue and Tiffin on his hind legs and started to gallop with the whole herd too, so already we are seeing a huge improvement. As he physically gets stronger, he is establishing greater respect within the herd, too. He is a huge asset to the team and adored by everyone. A true gentle giant.

ACKNOWLEDGEMENTS

The writing of this book was primarily a solitary process, but the overall result is a team effort. I am hugely grateful to everyone who provided input and support along the way, from the conception of the idea to the completed book.

Firstly, thank you Pepsi, my black Labrador, who sat with me in a field for four days. The output of that time was the title of this book. It was at least a start!

A huge thank you to the contributors to this book – Susan Gee from Yorkshire Water, Elizabeth Cronin from the New York State Office for Victim Services and Colin D. Smith, aka The Listener. Their contributions highlight practical examples of the concepts in this book, demonstrating their importance in different working environments.

The CEOs I interviewed for this book gave me their precious time and great insights into their worlds – Nigel Newton, Sue Noyes, Elizabeth Cronin, Sondra Scott, Gina Lodge, Bridget Shine, Peter Istead, Sue Grindrod, Nick Eastwood, Paul Faulkner and many others through more informal conversations. Many of them talked about the chapters in my book without having seen the table of contents, giving me confidence in my ideas before I started.

I continue to interview executives for a *Leading Through Uncertainty* podcast and their stories were invaluable in shaping the final book. Thank you also to my clients over the years. I have learned from each one, and it was an honour and a privilege to witness the depth of learning and to learn alongside them.

A team of mentors and support buddies helped me from start to finish. My writing buddies Wendy Prior and Rachael Beesley tolerated me for a week's writing retreat, during which I prevaricated and procrastinated while they got on with writing. They kicked me into action and got me off to a great start, despite my resistance. My book mastermind buddies Michael Brown, Elaine Halligan and Anne Archer challenged and supported me in equal measure throughout the writing process. Tom Evans provided guided meditations to help me find my flow whenever I got stuck, which was quite often.

Thank you to my publisher, Alison Jones of Practical Inspiration Publishing, who believed in me from the moment we met via Facebook. At the moments when I thought I might abandon the idea of writing this book, she knew I wouldn't. Her calm, deep faith in me kept me going. In particular, she helped me get unstuck when I hit a wall a week before the deadline.

I extend enormous gratitude to John Palmer, who beta read the first draft of this book in great detail, highlighting everything he disagreed with, as well as highlighting the parts he thought were great. John's incredibly thoughtful feedback gave me confidence in some of what I'd written and helped me turn the dodgy sections from a series of mutterings into the final book. This book would not have been published without John's attention to detail and his honest feedback. Gratitude doesn't come close. Thanks also to Dana Reynolds, who told me the book was needed and relevant, and helped me make the concepts come more alive as a result of her feedback.

Thank you to John Cleary for the photographs in the book and Jerry Longland for the illustrations. You are two people who continually provide support that is way beyond your remit.

To my husband Paul, who never complained as I spent long hours writing while he ran around after me and provided meals and lots of tea. After writing the first few chapters, I hit a wall, believing my writing to be a load of twaddle. Paul read the first few chapters, offered ideas to improve the book and convinced me to keep going.

Finally, I'm blessed to have the most incredible mentors in the form of my equine team – Kalle, Opus, Tiffin, Mr Blue and Gio. They may not have been much use in the writing process, but much of what I've learned about leading through uncertainty is as a result of working with them.

In the end, it was a team effort. I did the writing but the extensive conversations, learning, feedback and support shaped this book.

Thank you everyone. Here's to the next one!

ABOUT THE AUTHOR

Jude Jennison is a strategic leadership partner, international speaker and horse-assisted educator, specialising in leading through uncertainty. A business owner since 2010, Jude previously worked for IBM for 16 years, where she managed a budget of $1 billion and led UK, European and global teams.

Jude works with CEOs, executives, senior leaders and entrepreneurs to improve business results through strategic alignment and sustainable behavioural change.

She is author of the book *Leadership Beyond Measure*, in which she shares her extraordinary story of overcoming her lifelong fear of horses and providing Leadership with Horses workshops only eight months later.

She has been featured on BBC2's *Victoria Derbyshire* programme, BBC Radio 4 *You & Yours*, as well as being featured in the *Daily Telegraph, Financial Times, Virgin Entrepreneur* and many local radio interviews and press articles. Jude is the host of a podcast series called *Leading Through Uncertainty*, in which she interviews leaders on their experiences of uncertainty.

Married to Paul, who never wanted pets, Jude now owns five horses, two dogs and a cat. She lives in Warwickshire, UK and works all over the world, partnering with other practitioners to provide Leadership with Horses to international clients.

INDEX

A

acquisitions 99
action(s) 32, 51, 93–4, 130,
    147, 185, 192; *see also*
    inaction
adaptability 76, 135, 175, 190,
    202, 204; *see also* flexibility
adrenaline 63, 100, 192
agility 135, 204
Airbnb 29
alignment 161–2, 166–7, 179,
    188, 191
Amazon 29, 131
analysis paralysis 134–5
anger 47, 95, 99
anxiety 39–41, 64, 80, 115,
    191, 197–8, 201
approach 42, 60 75, 93–4,
    116, 118, 131, 134–5, 144,
    192–4, 201–2
artificial intelligence 30, 32
ask for help 8, 59–61, 164
attachment 75, 81–2, 189, 191,
    203–5
authentic behaviour 115
authentic leadership 199–201
authenticity 99, 201

B

balance 77, 148–9, 186
    balance of certainty and
        uncertainty 109–10
behaviour 3, 30, 51–2; *see also*
    learned behaviours
    authentic behaviour 115
    incongruent behaviour
        199–200
    stress behaviours 77
    default habits and
        behaviours 95, 201
    default patterns of
        behaviour 8, 93, 186
behavioural change 115, 132
beliefs 141–2, 149–50, 177, 190
Black, C. 65
blame 60, 64, 75, 80, 94–6,
    151, 164, 179, 187, 189,
    202, 206
boundaries 108, 111–12, 114,
    117–21
brain 5, 26, 28, 43, 61, 131, 201
Brexit 80
burnout 27, 63–4, 67, 69, 95,
    118, 192, 209

C

case study 13, 49, 83, 95, 116,
128, 178, 200, 208
CEOs, interviewing 2, 109–10,
146
certainty 60, 112, 118–21; *see
also* balance of certainty
and uncertainty
desire for certainty 77–81,
135
challenge 10, 41, 43–5; *see also*
uncertainty, challenge of
challenge the status quo 21
challenges 2–4, 94–5, 205
emotional challenges
11–12
change 51, 79–80, 98; *see also*
behavioural change
continuous change 131
fast-paced change 11, 20,
141
maturity to change 141
organisational change
64, 98–9
pace of change 26–32,
64, 66, 109
rapid change 98, 175
resistance to change 45,
77–8
technological change 31
chaos 108–9, 119, 188–9; *see
also* confusion
choice 115–16, 174–5, 177–8
imperfect choices 114
clarity 5–7, 110–14, 117–21,
189–91

clarity of direction 9
creating clarity 189–91
lack of clarity 42, 185
client(s) 4–7, 76, 148–9,
156–62
client case studies 13
client confidentiality 13,
124
client experiences 13
client team 49, 216
co-sensing and co-shaping the
future 123–37
Coaches Training Institute 20
coaching business 19–20
cognitive process(ing) 50, 130,
172, 202
collaboration 125–6, 141, 189
collaboration not competition
34–5
collective leadership 125–7, 204
comfort zone 8, 44–5, 74–5,
85, 98, 175–6, 185–6
command and control 76, 191,
203
communication 112, 124
advanced form of
communication 151
channels of
communication 176,
179
communication skills 21
non-verbal
communication 5
poor communication 150
community 28, 32–4, 43,
164–5

compassion 172–3, 194, 205–11

competition 34–5, 160; *see also* collaboration not competition

computers 28, 42, 217

confidence 44–5, 93–4, 124–6, 216–17; *see also* self-confidence

confidentiality 83, 96, 129, 178, 200, 208; *see also* client confidentiality

conflict 51, 82, 125, 143, 146–7, 160, 187–8

confrontation 74

confusion 9, 109, 111, 218

connecting in different ways 157–8

connection 32–6, 82–3, 117–18, 127–30, 155–67, 198–200

connection or disconnection 32–4

connection and support 155–67

conscious awareness 34

conscious decisions 93, 133

conscious leadership 217

consequences 4, 30, 48, 51, 64, 93

consideration 13, 69, 130

context of uncertainty *see* uncertainty

control 78, 130, 175, 190–1, 204, 213–14; *see also*

command and control; self-control

in control 7–8, 10–11, 78, 87, 184–5

let go of control 176, 198, 203, 210

losing control 50

out of control 47, 69, 92

conversation 127–8, 139, 142, 145, 151; *see also* difficult conversations

core of humanity *see* humanity

corporate social responsibility 66

courage 126, 178, 218–9

creativity 78, 109, 126, 130–1, 176, 189

critical thinking 42

criticism 64, 80, 115–6, 151, 164–5, 189, 202

Cronin, Elizabeth 100–1

culture 34, 48, 60, 64, 80, 84, 114, 130; *see also* fear culture; high-performing culture

culture change 98

culture of innovation 127

culture of trust 176

curiosity 4

D

deadline(s) 62, 203–4, 206

challenging deadlines 199

tight deadlines 26, 78

unrealistic deadlines 118, 207

decision(s) 28, 31, 43, 93, 133;
see also conscious decisions
effective decisions 46–7
Deloitte Global Human
Capital Trends report 30
dialogue 81–2, 139–41, 150–3,
189–90; see also listening
difference(s) 81–5, 143–4,
149–50, 161, 188–91
difficult conversations 147
Dines, Laurel 161–2
direction 110, 112, 121, 148–9
change direction 134
discomfort of uncertainty 78,
87, 110–11, 183–95
disconnection 32–6, 128, 134,
142–3, 186–8
disengagement 186–8
distraction 186, 194

E
ease 197–8, 204–5; see also flow
eco 125, 136
Edelman Trust Barometer
Report 146
ego 125–6, 186, 201
embodying uncertainty see
uncertainty
embracing differences 81–4
emergence 123
emotion(s) 5, 33–5, 46–53,
91–2, 99–100, 115, 176,
204, 219
suppressing emotions
46–8

unskilled usage of
emotions 46
emotional intelligence 32, 85,
219
emotional outbursts 80, 92, 99
emotional response(s) 84–5,
217
empathy 95–8, 100, 124, 140,
208
employee engagement 9
environment(s) 27, 84, 92–3,
107, 116–17, 130–2, 158,
179, 218, 225
listening to the
environment 146–8
working environment
59, 65, 82
Equine Guided Leadership 10,
21
equine team see meet the
equine team
ethical debate 32
ethics 30, 36
ethics of technology 30–2
expectations 68, 84, 108, 111,
159, 198–9, 207
experience 67, 116, 218
client experiences see
client experiences
embodied experience 5
human experience(s) 43,
46, 85, 96, 206, 209,
217
new experience 176, 201,
216

past experiences 12, 43, 89, 93–7, 191
exploration 10, 80, 85, 126, 191

F

failure 60–1, 94–5, 108, 206; *see also* fear of failure
Farmer, P. 66; *see also* Stevenson/Farmer report
fear 64, 73–86, 89–90, 108, 177, 187; *see also* polarisation
    fear culture 79
    fear of failure 48, 68, 74, 79, 204
    fear of horses 17–18, 21–23
    fear of uncertainty 20, 175
    fear of the unknown 80
    fear of vulnerability 176, 200
feedback 10, 42, 76, 116, 162, 201, 234–5
    non-judgemental feedback 5
    non-verbal feedback 8
feeling(s) 41–3, 50, 126–7, 143–4, 176; *see also* emotion(s)
felt sense 163
final thoughts 219–21
flexibility 76, 92, 110, 112, 130, 133, 135, 175, 204; *see also* adaptability
flow 20, 172, 199, 204–5

framework 107–21, 171, 204
frustration 47, 63, 76, 134, 165, 204
future of business 10, 48

G

Gee, Susan 65–7
Gio 12, 29, 39–41, 44–5, 155, 169–72, 216, 231–2, 235
global bank 46
global corporation 21
global economy 2, 84, 125, 133, 137
global ecosystem 141
global problems 2
global scale 1, 80
global teams *see* team(s), global
globalised workplace 190
goal(s) 82, 131, 206
    collective goals 147
    common goal 112, 161, 179
    end goal(s) 85, 96, 125, 128, 189, 205
    individual goals 192
    primary goal 6
    shared goal 81
    tangible goals 114
grip 8, 217
grounded *see* staying grounded
gut instinct 5, 7, 43, 142, 161, 200; *see also* intuition

H

harmony 124, 144, 188, 204
head, heart and gut 5, 51, 127, 149, 193; *see also* heart
health, 62; *see also* mental health; occupational health; World Health Organization
    emotional health 63, 206
    health implications 69
    ill health 64, 66
    physical health problems 64
    public health agenda 66
heart 34, 43, 84, 180
    following my heart 22–2
heart and soul, Leading from the 213–21
heroism 125
hierarchy 2, 5, 26, 42
high-performance culture 19–20, 27, 126–7, 175
high-performing team(s) 50, 83, 111, 225
HorseDream Partner 22
HSE 64
Hudson Talent Solutions 161–2; *see also* Dines, Laurel
human 41–3, 48, 203, 206, 217; *see also* superhuman
    being human 197
    human beings 25–30, 91, 101, 160, 209
    human capacity 28, 62
    human condition 89, 91, 204

human experience(s) 43, 46, 85, 96, 206, 209, 217
human species 217
humanity 30–2, 46, 48, 160, 206–9
    core of humanity 28, 91, 165

I

IBM 9, 19, 237
impact 31–2, 47, 50–1, 78, 91–4, 97–9, 115–16, 133–4, 142, 145, 158–9, 177
inaction 162
Industrial Age 29, 32
influence 44, 99
inner peace 19, 220
innovation 59–60, 78, 114, 127–8, 130–1, 151, 176, 189, 191, 206
insecurity 111
instincts 22, 135, 163
integrity 46, 79, 125, 201
intellect 5, 32, 219
intention(s) 145, 158, 165, 203
interaction 118, 158, 173–4, 180
intuition 22, 52, 163

J

judgement 75, 80, 95–6, 115–16, 151, 164, 179, 189, 202
    emotional judgement 43–6

K

Kalle 6, 17–19, 22–3, 58–9, 74, 95, 99, 113,126, 129–9, 139–40, 143, 155, 157, 162, 170, 183–5, 198–200, 208, 213–16, 216, 218, 220, 226–7, 229–30, 235

L

Leadership Beyond Measure 13, 18, 21, 77, 78, 98, 112, 144, 215, 237
leadership model 111–12
leading from behind 112
leading from the front 109, 112, 126
leading from the middle 112
leading through uncertainty white paper 10
leap of faith 61, 173
learned behaviours 90–1
learning 33, 93, 95, 115–16, 215–18
    disruptive learning 130
    experiential learning 132
    learning curve 21
    learning with horses 132, 218
    learning to listen 144–5
    online learning 132
letting go 115, 176, 191, 201–3
life expectancy 63
listening 81, 127, 139–49, 175, 205; *see also* dialogue
logic 7, 22, 40, 43

M

machine(s) 27–9, 61, 96, 206, 209, 217
macro 132–3, 136–7, 217; *see also* micro
masks 44, 175–8, 190, 199–200
mastering uncertainty *see* uncertainty, mastering
maturity to change *see* change, maturity to change
meaning 46, 50
meet the equine team 225–32
mental health 64–9, 206
Mental Health First Aid course 67
mental health issues 49, 61, 90, 93
mental health training 65
mergers 99
micro 132–3, 136–7, 217; *see also* macro
mistrust 99, 177–80
movement 134–5, 172
Mr Blue 12, 29, 155, 170, 216, 230–2, 235
multi-tasking 62
mutual respect 5–6, 144

N

needs 47–8, 62, 84–5, 117–18, 139–44, 148, 149
network and community 164–5
New York State Office of Victim Services 100–1

non-verbal *see* communication,
non-verbal; feedback,
non-verbal

O

occupational health 65, 67
opinions, diverse 33, 78, 81
opportunity 4–5, 8, 80, 85,
114, 142, 151, 160, 189, 218
Opus 12, 123–5, 156–7, 170,
228–9, 235
organisation(s) 26–7, 48–9,
62–9, 79–83, 114, 130–3,
209–10, 217
organisational trauma 98–101
overwhelm 26–7, 29, 61–70,
118, 130, 186, 192, 219; *see
also* stress

P

pace 34, 68, 77–8, 112, 116,
125, 127–30; *see also*
change, pace of
pain 89, 91–2, 94–5, 98; *see
also* trauma
paradigm shift 4, 175, 204
paradox 150, 188–9
partnership 5, 61, 214–15, 226
passion 213, 219–20
past experiences *see*
experiences, past
pause for breath 23, 200
people pleaser(s) 7, 148
performance coach 20

polarisation 73–86, 118, 130,
151, 217; *see also* fear;
polarities; paradox
polarities 188–9, 194–5; *see
also* paradox
possibility 21, 123
power 7, 125, 204, 220, 227–9;
see also processing power
power of connection
157–8
power struggle 228
pressure 27, 47–9, 62–4, 67–9,
77–9, 92–4, 161, 164–5,
198–9, 205–8
priorities 26
processing power 26–30, 57, 62
productivity 50, 68, 134
provoking personal insight 12,
37, 53, 71, 87, 103, 121, 137,
153, 167, 181, 195, 211
psychological assessments 42
purpose 46, 48, 110, 112, 117,
161–2, 213, 219
PWC, Annual CEO Survey 146

R

rapport, building 158–9
rational thought 42, 52
reasoning 7, 22, 40, 42–3, 172,
192; *see also* logic
recalibration 5
redundancy 64, 79, 92, 98–9
reflection 13, 27, 77–8, 82,
127, 136, 218; *see also* self-
reflection

relationship(s) 27, 48, 75–6,
83–4, 127–9, 139–44, 148–
9, 151–3, 160–1, 174–5,
177–80, 187, 189, 200
relationship skills 7
remote connections 163–4
research 2, 5, 30, 109, 193
resilience 34, 68–9, 92, 133, 217
resistance 45, 73–9, 176
resources, other 13
responsibility 3, 31, 68–9, 108,
187, 203; *see also* corporate
social responsibility
personal responsibility
108
social responsibility 32
take responsibility 51–2,
125, 165
restructuring 98
results 45–6, 77, 82–3, 124,
131, 139–40, 206–8
collective results 136
fast results 125
numerical results 27
righteous indignation 99, 165
risk(s) 2, 84, 113, 130, 132
robot(s) 12, 28, 42–3

S
safety 8, 70, 80, 111, 172–3,
177, 185
emotional safety 108
physical safety 61, 108
psychological need for
safety 21

Scott, Sondra 112–13
security 30, 111, 175
self-awareness 5, 39, 47, 51,
93, 114–16
self-belief 39, 45, 172
self-care 207–8
self-confidence 39
self-control 115–17
self-esteem 8
self-reflection 12
sensing from the wider field
130–2
shared leadership 2
skills 28, 109, 127, 130, 135,
188–9, 204
leadership skills 85, 220
negotiation skills 5
new skills 3, 92, 94, 218
relationship skills 7
slow down 29, 116, 127–9,
162, 193; *see also* speed up
small business 9, 20–1
Smith, Colin D. 144–6
social media 28, 33–5, 62, 186
society 2–3, 30–1, 34, 133,
217; *see also* corporate
social responsibility
speed 27–9, 116, 192
high speed 160
speed up 20, 29, 61, 127–9
status quo 20, 76–7; *see also*
challenge the status quo
staying grounded 191–3
Stevenson, D. 66; *see also*
Stevenson/Farmer report

Stevenson/Farmer report 65–6
strategic alignment 237
strategic foresight 132
strategic leadership partner
    4, 237
strategic vision 11
stress 45–6, 68–71, 91–3, 130–
    1, 176, 201, 203–6, 217; *see
    also* work-related stress
structure 9, 115, 118; *see also*
    support structure
struggle 114–15, 164, 197, 205;
    see also power struggle
supercomputers 25, 28, 230
superhuman 26, 28, 59, 207,
    209
support 8, 43–5, 59–61, 64–5,
    100–3, 112, 155–67
support structure 21, 109
sustainable future 31

T
targets 31, 93, 114, 206
    aggressive targets 3, 19, 27
    competing targets 82, 161
    financial targets 27, 83
    realistic targets 62, 70
    setting targets 84, 126
    stretch targets 20, 26, 203
    unrealistic targets 68, 208
task 128–9, 140, 148–9, 199;
    see also multi-tasking
team, aligned 82; *see also*
    client team; high-
    performing team

cohesive team 112
collective team 203
diverse teams 151
executive team(s) 221, 228
human team 6, 111, 170,
    225
Leaders by Nature team
    226, 231
team member(s) 76, 97,
    158
virtual teams 163
team-building events 162
teamwork 126, 208
technology 25–37, 61–3,
    163–4, 186, 193, 206, 217
tension 63, 80, 82, 116, 125,
    128, 146, 161, 203, 205
The Listener *see* Smith, Colin D.
thinking and feeling 41–3
thought leadership 28
Three Positions of Leadership
    112
Tiffin 40, 83, 89–90, 92, 96–7,
    143, 155, 170, 174, 178, 216,
    229–30, 232, 235
training 22, 69; *see also* mental
    health training
Trakehner 23, 226, 230–1
transparency 99, 115, 147,
    175, 179
trauma 12, 89–92, 95–103; *see
    also* organisational trauma
trust 150, 159–60, 169–81, 194,
    199; *see also* Edelman Trust
    Barometer Report; mistrust

U

Uber 29

uncertainty 1–13, 43–5, 59–61, 78–80, 91–2, 130–3, 201–5; *see also* balance of certainty and uncertainty; discomfort of uncertainty

challenge of uncertainty 3–4

context of uncertainty 15

embodying uncertainty 216–19

facing uncertainty head on 22–3

horses and uncertainty 4–8

mastering uncertainty 36, 53, 70, 86, 102, 120, 136, 152, 166, 180, 194, 210

path of uncertainty 17–23

staying with the discomfort of uncertainty 183–95

unconscious bias 82

unforeseen circumstances 135

unforeseen events 132

unknown 44, 61, 110–11, 199, 202, 216; *see also* fear of the unknown

unpredictability 4, 90

V

values 84, 113–20, 128, 141–2, 149–50, 179–80, 190–1

Values, needs and beliefs 149–50

Verisk Maplecroft 112; *see also* Scott, Sondra

Volini, E. 30

W

Walsh, B. 30

vulnerability 61, 111, 155, 160, 175–7; *see also* fear of vulnerability

WhatsApp 28, 34

Wheatley, Margaret 205

white paper 10, 13, 112

wisdom 142

collective wisdom 4

innate wisdom 35

Source of wisdom 48–51

wisdom of a wider system 131

Wisdom of fear 84–5

work-life balance 149

work-related stress 61–7, 98, 118

working with horses 5–6, 21, 73, 132, 148

workload 43, 57, 61–7, 95–8, 118, 160, 203, 206

workplace 2, 8, 46, 59, 63–7, 91, 117

workshop(s) 183–5, 219

World Health Organisation 65

Y

Yorkshire Water 65–7